Foundations of Music History

CARL DAHLHAUS

Foundations of
Music History

translated by
J. B. Robinson

CAMBRIDGE UNIVERSITY PRESS
Cambridge
London   New York   New Rochelle
Sydney   Melbourne

Published by the Press Syndicate of the University of Cambridge
The Pitt Building, Trumpington Street, Cambridge CB2 IRP
32 East 57th Street, New York, NY 10022, USA
296 Beaconsfield Parade, Middle Park, Melbourne 3206, Australia

Originally published in German as *Grundlagen der Musikgeschichte* by Musikverlag
Hans Gerig, Cologne, 1967 and © Laaber–Verlag
Dr Henning Müller-Buscher, 1982
First published in English by Cambridge University Press 1983 as
Foundations of Music History
English edition © Cambridge University Press 1983

Printed in Great Britain at the Pitman Press, Bath

Library of Congress catalogue card number: 82–9591

British Library Cataloguing in Publication Data
Dahlhaus, Carl
Foundations of music history.
1. Music – History and criticism
I. Title   II. Grundlagen der Musikgeschichte.
English
780'.9   ML160

ISBN 0 521 23281 3 hard covers
ISBN 0 521 29890 3 paperback

Contents

Contents

Translator's preface

Professor Dahlhaus has handled a complex topic with a light touch and enormous vitality, yet the English-speaking reader may find parts of his argument rather inaccessible. There is a simple reason for this: the author is building upon the philosophical tradition of German idealism, which not only developed independently of the Anglo-American analytic tradition but in many ways stands diametrically opposed to it. The reader of the German edition is likely to understand something more or less specific by the term *Verdinglichung*, a concept exhaustively analysed by Hegel, Marx and their successors. What, however, will the English-speaking reader make of its exact English equivalent, 'reification'? Probably nothing. Nor will it help if he has been trained in analytic philosophy, where this term serves entirely different purposes in contexts such as 'reification of universals'. The terminology of the German idealist tradition in philosophy has yet to find its way comfortably into our language. Entire families of concepts such as *Entäusserung, Verfremdung, Entfremdung, Vergegenständlichung* and the like, with all their many shades of meaning, have at one time or another been translated into that overworked and by now practically meaningless word 'alienation'. Even so fundamental a distinction as subject versus object has yet to take hold in our educated discourse: we refer to the 'subject' of contemplation, or the 'subject' of a study, where German speakers, relying on a distinction at least as old as Hegel, would use the word *Objekt,* reserving *Subjekt* for the person doing the contemplating or studying.

The English-speaking lay reader may well wonder why these difficult-sounding terms and distinctions have been brought to bear on music, or even on history. Shouldn't they be left in the more rarefied world of philosophy from which they come? The fact is that in Germany they have taken hold in a good many academic fields which stand well apart from philosophy. They have even found their way into the arts as well, Brecht's *Verfremdungseffekt* being just one example among many. So to help the reader of the English-language edition over some of the difficulties they may raise for him in this book, I offer the following brief explanation of some of the key terms in Professor Dahlhaus's argument.

The subject–object distinction is an appropriate starting point. It is of crucial significance to Hegel's epistemology, or theory of human knowledge. Before we can have knowledge of a thing we must first recognise that thing as being different from ourselves, i.e. as being an object. Otherwise we would not even be aware of its existence and there would be nothing to explain. In turning that entity into an object to be investigated we ourselves become a 'subject' in relation to that object, i.e. we become the agency doing the investigating and seeking comprehension. This is the process known as *Vergegenständlichung* or 'objectification'. The goal of knowledge is to reach an understanding of the object such that the condition of 'alienation' existing between subject and object is resolved, though of course on a higher plane than hitherto. This process is what Hegel called *Aneignung*, 'assimilation' or 'appropriation'. All acquisition of knowledge follows, indeed must follow, this underlying pattern of objectification and assimilation.

Now Hegel was a systematic philosopher of the sort not generally encouraged in our Anglophone tradition. Granted that the subject–object distinction is fundamental to human knowledge, it seemed reasonable to him to conclude that it must also underlie the fields of which human knowledge is possible. In history, the subject–objective distinction had for Hegel a threefold relevance. First, the individual historical agent acts as a subject insofar as he transforms his wishes, desires or intentions – what German idealists called his 'will' – into deeds. This is the process known as *Entäusserung* – 'externalisation' or 'concretisation'. These deeds then become 'objects', and stand in the same relation of alienation to the historical agent as do objects of knowledge to the cognitive faculties of the subject. They too must be assimilated and the condition of alienation resolved if the agent is to understand himself in relation to his world.

History acquires a subject in a second sense when it is written down, namely in the sense implied when we say that history is a 'subjective' discipline. Here the historian becomes the subjective agency, and the events of history (including the individual 'subjects' of the historical agents) become the 'objects' of his investigation. The facts and personages, events and structures of history become objects in the epistemological sense described above, and are objectified and assimilated in the same fundamental way as all other human knowledge.

Yet there is a third sense in which history has a subject. As the individual participating agents in history commit their deeds and create their artifacts it soon becomes clear that larger patterns are established over which none of them, taken individually, has any control. The emergence of national characters, the creation of classes, the changing demographic complexion of a nation – these things are not willed by any one subjective historical agent, nor are they present in the minds of any but a few of the more far-sighted contemporary participants. Yet these large historical phenomena also exist as historical fact, and must be comprehended by the historian. Indeed, it is not far wrong to say that comprehending them is his principal task. They are, then, objects. Do they have a corresponding subjective agency which summoned them into existence, just as historical deeds are summoned into existence by their perpetrators? To Hegel there was only one answer: Yes. And this subjective agency became, in his philosophy of history, that much misunderstood figure, the *Weltgeist* – the 'world mind' or 'world spirit' standing over lesser subjective agencies such as the *Nationalgeist* and *Zeitgeist* and realising its will in the history of nations. To elucidate the workings of this world spirit (a later generation might have called it the 'collective consciousness') is the historian's main task, and it is in this sense that Professor Dahlhaus asks, as he does in chapter 4, 'Does music history have a subject?'.

Where does this leave music? Music historians are, of course, historians like any others, and must confront the past and its threefold subjectivity like their colleagues in other branches of history. Their field is, however, complicated by the nature of music as an art. In one respect, composers behave as historical agents in the normal sense of the term. After all, they too transform their intentions into deeds and artifacts, namely into works of music; they also take part in the historical events of their own time. However, composers are also subjects in quite another sense, namely in the sense implied when we speak of the 'meaning' of a piece of music or say that the composer is 'speaking to us'. Works of music, or at least great works of music, are not irrevocably consigned to the past like historical events, but have a prolonged afterlife during which they change character, acquire and discard meaning, and influence the further progress of the art. In this subsequent history of a work, its so-called *Wirkungsgeschichte,* the composer remains as a subjective agency behind his work. But how, and in what sense? This is only one question among many that Professor Dahlhaus poses and explores in his attempt to unravel the intricate relation between the music historian and his complicated subject (or, as should now be clear, his 'object') – music.

This is, of course, no more than a thumbnail sketch of the philosophical background to Professor Dahlhaus's book; but it may serve to bridge the gap between the English-speaking student of music and his German counterpart, who would immediately cut through the philosophical jargon to recognise Professor Dahlhaus's concerns for the pressing issues that they are. Throughout my translation I have assumed that the reader knows nothing beyond hearsay of the German idealist tradition. All philosophical terms, whether the aforementioned epistemological ones, Dilthey's *Lebensphilosophie*, the *Verstehen* theory of history or Windelband's 'nomothetic' and 'idiographic' disciplines, are glossed at their first occurrence wherever they have not been glossed in the original German. I have taken pains to render the philosophical passages into non-technical language as far as possible. Theses and antitheses are not 'sublated' but 'resolved' into syntheses, and *Empirie* is not 'empiricism' (which means something quite different in Anglophone philosophy) but 'the quantitative method' or, simply, 'statistical tables'. A problem was posed by the use of *Form* and *Inhalt*, which in German mean something different from 'form' and 'content' in English and which I have rendered as 'technique' and 'expression'. I have also retained Professor Dahlhaus's many references to Western art music as 'artificial music', which should be taken in the literal sense, i.e. a music made up of artifices. The relatively new fields of *Rezeptionsgeschichte* and *Wirkungsgeschichte* have not yet found their way into Anglo-American academic parlance, but as it is merely a matter of time before they do I have avoided circumlocution and written simply 'reception history' for both. Where *Wirkungsgeschichte* alone is intended I have written of the 'subsequent history' of a work, meaning subsequent to its composition. I have taken the liberty of translating all quoted material anew.

I wish to extend my special thanks to Professor Dahlhaus for encouraging me to undertake this translation and to the publishers for their patience in seeing it into print. Mr Neil Mackenzie of Glasgow read the entire manuscript at an early stage, offering innumerable helpful and thought-provoking comments, as did the publishers' subeditor Ms Ruth Smith, who combines the two admirable virtues of an inquiring mind and a layman's intolerance of waffle. Needless to say, the final decision in all matters of translation rested with me, and such blemishes as exist in the translation are my own doing. My wife Judith helped with the proofreading and preparation of the index; for this, and for many other things too, my heartfelt thanks.

Munich, April 1982   J. B. Robinson

Foreword

Foundations of Music History is a presumptuous title. I would therefore ask the reader to bear in mind that it represents a makeshift solution to the problem of finding a more precise and less bombastic one. As compensation for my failure, or at least in an attempt to make it pardonable, all I can offer is a few admonitory assurances. The following historiographical reflections, which were occasioned, or rather provoked, by the obvious and disproportionate lack of theory in my own peripheral discipline as compared to the veritable welter of theoretical writing in general history, sociology and epistemologically orientated philosophy, are not meant to be an introduction to the basic facts of music history. Nor are they intended as a textbook of historical method in the manner of Bernheim's work. Still less do they constitute a philosophy of history or an ideological critique in the respective traditions of Hegel and Marx. Their closest model might be Johann Gustav Droysen's unsurpassed lecture series of 1857, *Historik*.

It is difficult, however, not to become involved with Marxist ideological critique, since in this field of study – or at least in the field it claims to study – choosing a topic is always inextricably bound up with deciding in favour of one of the various contesting positions it encompasses. Suppose, for instance, that we were to make the seemingly innocuous remark that our concern was not the sociology but the logic of history, thereby insisting on a distinction between a sociology of knowledge that pursues extrinsic relationships and a theory of history that examines intrinsic connections. To a Marxist – in whose eyes the only alternative to overt bias is covert bias – this would look suspiciously like a conservative stance entrenched behind formal argument. This suspicion cannot be allayed; it must simply be borne. At best we might rejoin that the history of scholarship has not yet succeeded in unearthing any connections between methodological precepts and political implications which are as clear-cut in practice as they are in theory. To maintain that structural history, for example, is *a priori* more 'progressive' than a history of events would be absurd in view of the work of Jacob Burckhardt or Wilhelm Heinrich Riehl. The alleged 'reactionary' nature of Russian formalism or Czech structuralism has been revealed as a falsification of the facts. And the dubious

I

method of understanding history by the process called *Verstehen* (lit. understanding, but here direct identification with historical agents) is not simply a matter of antiquarian posturing or escapist immersion in the past; on the contrary, it can be reconciled with a detached approach in which the past appears progressively more enigmatic and alien the better it is understood – or in which, to put it paradoxically, distance increases with proximity.

For decades now historians have been talking about a crisis in historical thought. At first, from Ernst Troeltsch in his *Der Historismus und seine Probleme* (1922) to Alfred Heuss's *Verlust der Geschichte* (1959), this crisis was seen and lamented not as a menace to the science of history from within – with doubt being cast on its underlying premises, its avowed goals and the measures taken to reach them – but as a disintegration of the role that history had once played in the popular imagination. In recent years, however, it has become increasingly apparent that the difficulties of principle in which history found itself embroiled were not so remote from the daily business of scholarship as historians once believed, or tried to believe – trusting in the distinction between a *métier* which one more or less mastered and a *Weltanschauung* which was one's private affair. If I may be permitted a digression into the personal by way of illustration: the following chapters from a philosophy of music history are the reflections of someone directly involved in the field and not those of a philosopher standing 'above it all'. They arose not from ambitious theoretical lucubration but from the practical difficulties that I encountered in trying to devise a history of nineteenth-century music.

1

Is history on the decline?

For several decades now historians have felt threatened by a loss of interest in history, even believing at times that their existence as an institution is in jeopardy. History – memory made scientific – is apparently no longer the primary authority that we turn to for guidance or support when trying to understand ourselves or the world we live in. In the nineteenth and early twentieth centuries it was taken for granted that we had to know the origins of a thing in order to know its essence. By now, however, this basic tenet has forfeited much of its credibility.

Prevailing opinion or prejudice as to the usefulness or the drawbacks of political history (which forms the main bone of contention) does not directly involve music history, however, as the two fields apparently draw on fundamentally different assumptions – though not even music history can escape the current intellectual fashion of having history take a back seat to sociology. Music histories have always been ambiguous in function. Sometimes they are read less as accounts of some aspect of the past than as historical commentaries to particular works – or, to put it bluntly, as concert or opera guides. Far from dismissing this practice as a mere abuse we should recognise in it a sign of the special nature of music historiography. For if we accept that the subject matter of music history is made up primarily, if not exclusively, of significant works of music – works that have outlived the musical culture of their age – and consequently that the aesthetic presence of individual works will necessarily intervene in any account of the past (whether as a selection criterion or as a factor in helping us decide what we want to know about), it then follows that an account of the origins and later history of musical works will serve a dual function, illuminating the preconditions for a given work on the one hand and on the other shedding light on the implications of the present-day listener's relation to that work. (The later history of a work – its *Wirkungsgeschichte* – is in turn the pre-history of its current reception.) We arrive at a better understanding of a thing, whether it be a piece of music or our own relation to that piece, by knowing the history behind it.

'That which was', writes Johann Gustav Droysen in his *Historik*, 'does not attract our interest simply because it was, but rather because, in a certain sense, it still is, in that it still exercises an influence' (p. 275). Seen in this light, a piece of written history, if it is to do justice to its subject, must take its character from the manner in which the object under discussion 'in a certain sense'. . . still is' – whether as a mere inference from present modes of behaviour or institutions, as a work performed in concert halls, or as a museum piece. A music historian who does not want to demean his subject can ill afford to overlook the current aesthetic presence of some of the works he wishes to put into an historical context. It would be unrealistic and absurd in the extreme for him to treat the musical past as though, like the political past, it was at best indirectly preserved in current events and affairs as a sort of proto-history to them. Music of the past belongs to the present as music, not as documentary evidence. This implies nothing less than that when we delve into the turmoil of current events to determine the function of music history we are not entirely beholden to vacillating opinions as to the value of recollecting the past. Music historiography has a different legitimation from political historiography. It differs from its political counterpart in that the essential relics that it investigates from the past – the musical works – are primarily aesthetic objects and as such also represent an element of the present; only secondarily do they cast light on events and circumstances of the past. It would be a patent caricature to compile a history of music strictly along the lines of political history, treating the score of, say, the Ninth Symphony as a document to be weighed alongside other pieces of evidence in reconstructing the events surrounding its première or some later performance. This is not to say that 'events' are irrelevant, merely that the emphasis falls on understanding works – which, unlike the relics treated in political histories, are the goal of historical inquiry and not its point of departure. The concept 'work', and not 'event', is the cornerstone of music history. Or, to put it in Aristotelian terms, the material of music history resides not in *praxis*, or social action, but in *poiesis*, the creation of forms.

The historian who takes the aesthetic presence of musical works as his point of departure does not necessarily overlook or belittle his distance from them in time, as the New Criticism has been faulted for doing. Indeed, ever since Schleiermacher it has been the fundamental axiom of historical hermeneutics (the science of interpretation) that surviving texts, whether musical or linguistic, remain partially obscure after an initial naive reading and do not disclose their full meaning until their historical preconditions and implications have been thoroughly analysed. The task of historical hermeneutics is to make alien material comprehensible, i.e. material that is remote in time or in social or ethnic origin. In so doing, we do not deny its extrinsic or intrinsic distance from us, but instead make this distance part of the process of perceiving the material in the context of the present as opposed to viewing it from a detached historical standpoint. In other words, an aesthetic presence based on such historical insight embraces rather than bypasses an awareness of this otherness or alienness. Admittedly the outcome of historical exegesis can never be entirely subsumed in aesthetic perception; yet a certain degree of mediation between the two is distinctly possible, and at all events less difficult than it might seem to the proponents of the aesthetics of immediacy, who regard the roundabout paths trodden by the historian as mere divagations. (This school fails to note that the aesthetic immediacy it insists upon can also be a secondary immediacy, as indeed it must be when dealing with complex or temporally remote works.) The knowledge that two and a half centuries lie between us and the completion of the St Matthew Passion does not impair our aesthetic appreciation of the work in the least, but rather forms a part of it. (However, one should take care not to confuse or equate historical insight that merges into aesthetic insight with that vague sense of temporal remoteness that so often pervades and tempers our perception of early music. A sense of nostalgia may possibly kindle an interest in history; but it can only hinder this interest by making further refinements by increased knowledge appear not just unnecessary but even harmful.)

Thus there is a fundamental difference between music history and political history, between the historical interpretation of an object which resides primarily in an aesthetic presence and the reconstruction of a past event which survives merely on the basis of its implications. This has not, however, prevented musicologists from developing an aversion to history, a mixture of suspicion and nervous uneasiness toward the time-honoured view that the principal concern of musicology is music history. It is not out of place here to examine the causes for this change in attitude and the arguments used in support of it. Indeed, the author of a treatise on music historiography is bound to devote particular attention to the difficulties he encounters.

Recent developments in music and a growing trend toward ideological critique have tended to cast increasing doubt on the premise that the concept 'work' is the central category of music, and hence of music historiography as well. On the one hand, 'open' forms have arisen in which the listener may no longer simply listen to the music as a passive agent, following its course in his mind, but is required to take an active part in creating it. On the other hand, suspicions are being aroused against the phenomena of 'alienation' (*Entfremdung*) and 'reification' or 'objectification' (*Verdingli-chung*). These two developments converge in the belief that, in music, the 'fixed letter' capable of being passed down to posterity is less important than the actual musical process, which we might describe as the 'event' that emerges partly from the written com-position, partly from its realisation in performance and partly from the modes of musical perception, with these three factors interac-ting on equal terms so that performer and listener are no longer subjected to the tyranny of the composer. (Referring to the 'auth-ority' of a work is taken as a sign of 'bad faith'.)

If drawn rigorously – as is hardly possible at present – the conse-quences for music historiography that would ensue from discarding the concept of 'work' would be practically inconceivable in scope. Luckily, it is not difficult to point out a few deficiencies in the historiographical thesis that musical processes have primacy over musical works. To begin with, it is a cardinal philosophical error to equate 'alienation' cursorily with 'objectification', i.e. with the re-alisation of a composer's intention in a concrete work or text, for the entire matter hinges precisely on discerning the slight but cru-cial difference in meaning between the philosophical and sociological uses of these terms – between *Vergegenständlichung* and *Verdinglichung*. Secondly, it is scarcely conceivable how an his-torian could ever succeed in reconstructing a bygone musical event – a complex interaction of text, performance and reception – to a degree of refinement that would not pale drastically beside a musical analysis of the work. A third objection is that 'open' forms are no more capable than 'closed' ones of being generalised into a principle that would encompass and govern the whole of music history. While it cannot be denied that 'music' and 'work' in the strong sense have not always been identical, there is no call to de-preciate the artificial music of post-medieval Europe – which is unquestionably rooted in the notions of 'work' and 'text' – or to

level accusations of provinciality against historians who have experienced the aesthetic presence of these works and see in them the
bedrock of music history. The musical 'work' as re-created in the
mind of the listener has a legitimate claim to existence as music,
and is not an inferior sub-species abstracted from the musical 'process'.

2

This waning of interest in history does not, or does not always,
imply a suspension of the 'historical awareness' that came to the
fore as a mode of thinking in the nineteenth century. On the contrary, the conviction that mental and social phenomena are 'historical through and through' is still very much with us, even among
some of those who decry history as an antiquarian science of the
past. We might almost speak of historicism without history, the
historical aspect being taken to reside solely in the element of
mutability. However, this would mean sacrificing the premise
which underlies traditional historical writings: that insight into
what something is arises from knowledge of how it came about. The
emphasis is placed not on the affirmative aspect of 'historicity',
whereby the past functions as the foundation and cornerstone of
the present, but on its critical aspect, on the implication that states
of affairs, to the extent that they have arisen historically as opposed
to being given by nature, can be altered or even undermined.

The analysis of the past in order to determine what is by virtue of
what has come about would then be replaced by an orientation
toward a utopian future – a 'real utopian future', as Ernst Bloch
would put it – with historical awareness always being understood as
an awareness of mutability. The thesis that has hitherto guided
traditional historical writings would be confronted by an antithesis
positing that what something 'is' is determined less by the origins it
has left behind than by the aggregate of possibilities it contains.
The deciding factor would no longer be what that something used
to be, but what it is capable of becoming.

Seen in these terms, history might simply be discarded as superfluous or, at best, reduced to a process of scanning the present in
the hope of descrying the vague outlines of a more perfect future.
The arsenal of history would be rummaged in search of constituent
parts to shore up or illustrate a particular vision of the future.
Objects hitherto lost in a corner would be seized upon by utopian
awareness and suddenly invested with far-reaching significance.

Homely introductions, unlikely transitions and codettas – in effect, musical passages that had hitherto rested in obscurity – figure in the vision of an unfettered music such as Ferruccio Busoni outlined in his *Entwurf einer neuen Aesthetik der Tonkunst* and in the theory of musical prose that Schoenberg advanced in his essay 'Brahms the Progressive'. In both cases these passages are meant to foreshadow a future state in which music, instead of conforming to heteronomous rules, will attain its true essence. (Modern revolutionaries differ from rebels of earlier centuries in that they are 'historicists': they consider history 'producible' and proceed from the premise that religion, culture and the state – Jacob Burckhardt's 'three potencies' – are 'historical through and through' to the conclusion that the mutability spoken of by historians can also be put into practice. The opposite pole to this revolutionary 'historicism' is the traditionalism of the conservatives, with their devotion to 'established truths', which are not only held to be true by virtue of being established but are also given the honour of always having been true simply because they happen to apply now.)

3

But shifting the emphasis of the font of 'historical awareness' from the past to the future is not only a clear indication that history is being subordinated to politics; it also conveys a mistrust of what earlier historians had agreed upon as constituting what 'belongs to history'. A sense of animosity towards the 'great men' who were once said to 'make history' is the natural counterpart of a sympathy for the masses who stood in their shadow, obliged to bear the burden of history.

In music history this change of perspective means that it is no longer merely the 'great works' towering above the rest of music's copious output that belong to history in the strict sense of the word. This status also accrues to the vast amounts of 'trivial music' that in fact go to make up the bulk of day-to-day musical reality, and should not therefore be summarily dismissed as the rubble that remains after the edifice of history has been erected. A piece of trivial music, so the argument goes, should not be regarded and evaluated as a 'work'; and any aesthetic or compositional analysis of such a piece amounts to a basic misunderstanding of the nature of this genre. Rather, music of this sort should be treated as a fragment of social reality, as a participating element within a social process or state. To put it another way, histories of musical works or compositional techniques based on the post-medieval concept of art must be replaced (the more conciliatory spokesmen of this view would say 'augmented') by social histories that explain musical creations in terms of their functions.

Yet to claim that 'greatness' in music is as insidious and ambivalent as its political counterpart, being a greatness for which other historical agents have had to pay the price, is to miss the point. No-one had a burden to bear because Beethoven wielded authority in music. This line of argument directed at 'great men' collapses when transferred from political tò music history. Moreover, it is a methodological solecism to mingle or confuse normative judgments (postulates as to what ought to be) with descriptive ones (knowledge of what used to be). Agreed, in the future it may be morally advisable, perhaps even unavoidable, to devote less time to the search for outstanding composers than to the development of a musical mass 'culture' deserving of the name; but it is also an incontrovertible fact that European music history since the Renaissance has advanced under the banner of what Alfred Einstein once used as a book title – 'Greatness in Music'.

Whether an historian elects to write a history of musical works and compositional technique as opposed to a social or functional history of music does not entirely depend on his own perception of the subject matter, which is a purely personal affair, even though it, too, can be influenced by external motives. Rather, this decision is, at least in part, predetermined by the nature of the subject under study, by the 'givens' of music. Whether and to what degree a stylistic or a social history of music or some reconciliation of the two (which, however, will have to favour one approach at the expense of the other) is appropriate to a particular fragment of musical reality will vary according to the period, field or genre studied. In principle there is nothing that will not submit to one or other of these approaches: granted the necessary degree of aesthetic insensitivity it is possible to analyse a piece of juke-box music in terms of its intrinsic value as a work or, alternatively, to reduce a Bach cantata to its role in the liturgy, i.e. to insist that the one represents a musical text and the other served a function. Yet scholarly experience has shown that it is possible in virtually every instance to determine to the satisfaction of everyone concerned whether a particular result is interesting and relevant or weak and misguided.

The problem of determining in what way the few successful trivial pieces differ from the numberless others that disappear

almost in the instant of their creation will hardly be solved by
technical arguments abstracted from artificial or pedagogical
music. Nor will an exclusively functional interpretation of a Bach
cantata account for the historical fact – which no historian,
however much inclined to favour antiquarian reconstructions, can
afford to ignore – that Bach's works were not only amenable to
reinterpretation in the nineteenth century to become the quintessence and paradigm of absolute music, but also, by virtue of this
reinterpretation, attained an historical importance unimagined by
Bach's eighteenth-century contemporaries. It was not until they
had undergone this profound alteration in their significance that
they were, so to speak, 'discovered' – though any historian who
shies away from the dogmatics of historical theory will be hard put
to decide whether what was discovered was in fact their 'real'
nature or a distortion of it.

One way of alleviating this methodological controversy would
appear to lie in measuring the two conflicting approaches in mixtures of varying strengths against the historical subject under
discussion instead of issuing claims of universality and carrying on a
feud in the abstract, fraught with ideological accusations of 'pre-
tentious elitism' or 'overbearing philistinism'. This is not to say that
the battle of principles should be abandoned: any attempt at ap-
peasement that glosses over the basic differences between the two
approaches would be not merely wrongheaded but doomed to
failure. But the controversy will remain pointless until it can draw
upon those practical examples and experiences without which proposed scholarly theories are as devoid of meaning as are mere
numbers in statistical tables. At the moment the advocates of a
sociological approach to the historiography of music are still
largely basking in their unfair advantage of being able to criticise
the deficiences of traditional music history instead of having to
justify their own results, which are far too few. But, of course, the
triumphs of programmatic historians over their more practically
minded colleagues have seldom been lasting.

4

The concept of continuity – the principal basis for writing history
in narrative form – has fallen into disrepute at the hands of sceptical
historiologists. True, those historians who have thought seriously
about their own discipline have always recognised the problems
that lurk when history is cast in narrative terms. Droysen was the

most outspoken proponent of the view that historical processes can never be reconstructed in full detail as they actually occurred. He reproached narrative history, as represented by Ranke, for conjuring up the 'illusion . . . that we are faced with an unbroken continuum of historical material, a unified chain of events, motives and aims' (*Historik*, p. 144). Yet this fictitious continuum, borrowed from the novel and put to use in full awareness of the actual inconsistency of surviving facts, is not the crucial point. Nineteenth-century historians, Droysen no less than Ranke, distinguished between a 'reality' that remains in part unaccounted for even after the most stubborn efforts have been made to reconstruct it, and a 'truth' of history that imparts sense and structure to what are otherwise mere accumulations of facts. If the idea of 'humanity' or the 'national spirit' is taken to be the motivating force behind history, the facts tend to fall into place practically of their own accord, forming a picture of historical development that owes its consistency less to the interaction of the particular facts involved than to the 'internal bond' that links the meanings behind them. When it is presented in terms of traditional modes of narration, i.e. those not yet influenced by Proust and Joyce, a fragment of the past is conveyed either by means of an illusory unbroken chain of processes or, more significantly, on the basis of the historian's preconceived liking for a particular 'idea', which then serves to distinguish the essential from the inessential and to give form to the chaos of empirical reality. (When Arthur C. Danto speaks in his *Analytical Philosophy of History* of an 'explanation sketch' that guides the historian, he is replacing the idea believed in – the 'truth' of history – by an heuristic model whose usefulness is in inverse proportion to the violence done to the facts by aligning them into a comprehensible pattern. Metaphysics deflates into mere methodology.)

However, when we surrender the ideas whose realisation was once thought to make history intelligible, the continuity or inner cohesion of events disintegrates, with the result that we can no longer substantiate our decisions as to what does or does not 'belong to history'. Yet it looks as though this controversy can be, if not settled, at least ameliorated by conferring relative rather than absolute validity upon the key principles, with empirical confirmation stepping in to fill the gap left by their weakened claims to universality.

Now a music history that proceeds from a study of musical works – even if more is said of the composers, whose biographies are scoured for explanatory matter, than of the music itself – is based on the notion of the autonomy of art, which plays the same role of an 'explanation sketch' as does the concept of national spirit in political histories. By drawing on the principles of novelty and originality – as they tend to do as if there were no possible room for contradiction – music historians present the evolution of music as an account of the origins of autonomous and unreduplicatable works of art, born of themselves and existing entirely for their own sakes. And the correlative to a history of works is a history of compositional technique or 'musical logic', meaning thematic and motivic manipulation, developmental variation and the construction of subtle yet far-reaching harmonic and tonal relations. This sort of music history treats the emergence and evolution of the devices that justify music's autonomy, its claim to be listened to for its own sake.

The idea that a musical work 'belongs to history' by virtue of its novelty, 'history' here being understood to mean a sequence of changes, is as seldom aired as it is constantly practised. Yet detractors of traditional music historiography who are well versed in the philosophy of history recognise in this tenet the error of blindly elevating an eighteenth- and nineteenth-century aesthetic premise – namely the belief that a work must be original to be authentic – to the status of a principle governing the whole of music history. Medieval music, the argument continues, has been distorted and put in a false perspective by an historiographical method that takes the novel or innovatory aspects of a particular decade or century as its primary historical substance in order to contrive a narrative history from the resultant succession of changes. While this criticism does not deny that innovation played a part in twelfth- or thirteenth-century musical culture (although strictly speaking we have no right to isolate and collect those phenomena that we happen to consider 'musical'), it does insist that the degree of innovation was never as significant as is suggested by histories based on nineteenth-century historiological precepts.

Any attempt to write history so as to place the stresses just as they existed in the minds of the participating historical agents, or rather of the influential groups among them, would mean replacing the customary depiction of events or works in series by descriptions of circumstances superseding one another, existing side by side or merging into one another. A history of works – which is only recognisable as such by its dependence on the novelty principle – would be suppressed in favour of a cultural history in which old and new combine, yielding images of the past in which certain configurations of then current ideas and ways of thinking, institutions and creations are deemed 'representative' and placed in the foreground accordingly.

A similar objection to that facing the history of works can also be raised against its near relation, the history of compositional techniques. Here, to gain a principle for selecting and linking facts, the focus is the emergence of 'musical logic' – the various technical devices that serve to justify artificial music in its claim to self-sufficiency, i.e. its absolution from extramusical function. No-one would seriously dispute the claim that the emergence and refinement of the structural potentials of tonality and thematic or motivic manipulation formed the pivotal historical process of the eighteenth and nineteenth centuries, an emphasis rooted in the aesthetic bias of that age towards works. However, it is not so clear to what extent historians of earlier epochs are warranted in making the development of structures and artistic devices their main concern: histories based on the premises of the fifteenth century, for example, might prefer to play down the techniques that enabled the polyphonic mass to attain cyclic unity as a work of art independent of a liturgical context and instead stress the elements that led a certain alliance of extramusical function and musical technique to crystallise into a norm for this genre – except of course in works whose ceremonial purposes called for that *ostentatio ingenii* ('flaunting of genius') that Glarean criticised in Josquin.

It remains uncertain, however, to what extent an historian should regulate his selection and ordering of facts to conform to the modes of thought and habitual patterns of outlook that reigned in the age he wishes to depict. In an extreme case this would lead to the dubious consequence – demanded by Hegel's argument that *res gestae* or 'human exploits' only become historical in the strict sense when made part of a *historia rerum gestarum* or 'history of human exploits' – of disregarding all epochs that had no awareness of history, i.e. ages of unbroken traditionalism to whom the present was nothing more than a repetition of the past. In these terms, a history founded on archaeology and drawing upon relics instead of records could never be more than a mere proto-history.

In addition to the general difficulties described above that seem to beset historiography as a whole there are others that are obviously specific to music history. In recent decades the concept of 'style' and the historical method based upon it have fallen by the wayside, kindling no spectacular controversies en route and leaving behind nothing but the husks of the various ideas associated with this term

in the early part of our century. However, as reflecting on history
also involves reflecting on the historical nature both of this subject
itself and of the procedures used to give it concrete form, it is not out
of place here to examine the reasons for the downfall of the 'history
of style' and reconstruct the problems that Guido Adler and Hugo
Riemann were trying to solve when they conceived this sort of
history; for, more likely than not, these problems are less transient
than the various answers they have been given over the years.

The crucial difficulty in defining style obviously lies in reconciling, without contrivance, the contradiction that even though
each complex of stylistic characteristics is supposed to be self-contained and intrinsically intelligible, we nevertheless determine a
style by comparing it with other styles and letting the traits that
differ serve as its defining features. Without plunging through the
thicket of competing definitions of style – that is, without having to
confront the underlying problems – it is nevertheless possible at
least to outline a few causes for the disintegration of the concept of
'style'. Hence I shall not discuss this concept itself so much as its
supposed relevance for the writing of history.

I

When Guido Adler proposed his theory of musical style in 1911 (in
Der Stil in der Musik) he drew on what Erich Rothacker later called
the 'organism model'. However treacherous this approach has
proved to be, it seems virtually indispensable for compiling histories from musical facts that have been determined on the basis of
style criticism. (As recently as 1965, for example, Edward A. Lippman could write first of a 'surprising analogy between the history
of a style and the life of an organism', only to emphasise later their
substantial dissimilarity and to propose that their resemblances
should form the object, and not the premise, of inquiry.[1]) According to Adler the 'style of a period, a school, an artist or work' does
not come about 'by chance, as a mere contingency to the artistic
will manifested therein, but rather is grounded on the laws of
origin, growth and decline found in organic evolution' (p. 13). Thus
Adler raises an analogy – which however permissible as a metaphor
makes a dubious historiographical theorem – to the status of a 'law'
governing music history. When it is viewed from the standpoint of
its methodological function, however, this naive metaphysic proves
to be anything but a mere chance deficiency that could be removed

[1] 'Stil', p. 1317.

without substantially altering the notion of a history of style. On the contrary, the analogy is an integral part of the argument: to determine a style – whether of an individual piece, a composer's life-work or the output of an entire period – we must first take a corpus of mutually incompatible, self-contained complexes and interlink them 'from without' by resorting to the organism model before they can even begin to appear as stages in an evolution. Of course, it is always possible to bracket adjacent stylistic complexes within some more comprehensive unit of measure designed for this purpose; but the resulting pyramid of stylistic concepts cannot easily be transformed into a picture of an evolutionary process. When Adler referred to the juxtaposition of styles in works as '*disjecta membra* of a pseudo-history' (p. 239) he put his finger squarely on the weak point of his own conception, merely failing to note that the problem he had pinpointed so clearly also occurs – on a different scale but unchanged in essence – with regard to the styles of an epoch.

2

It is no coincidence that the organism model – the prerequisite for writing history on the basis of style criticism – is inseparable in Adler's writings from an aesthetic bias towards classical styles:

In the course of the origin, flowering and decline of a style, the intermediate period invariably serves as the principal basis of comparison. Stylistic criteria are drawn from this middle period, e.g. from the style of the tenth and eleventh centuries in the case of plainsong, or the fully mature styles of the fifteenth and sixteenth centuries in the case of *a cappella* polyphonic music. At the same time, the significance and relevance of preliminary stages and later offshoots can, and indeed must, be recognised, even if at times they are at variance with certain crucial determinants of the style. A case in point is the early species of plainsong with interpolated notes, or the increasingly monorhythmic chant of the waning (or subsequent) periods, as compared to the mainstream of diatonic chant. Another example, from vocal polyphony, is the accessory or subsidiary application of instruments in the early stages, or the instrumental filler parts found in the later periods, as opposed to the strict adherence to the human voice during the period of maturity (*Methode der Musikgeschichte*, pp. 20f).

The language that Adler speaks as an historian betrays the classicism he clings to as an aesthetician. On the other hand, one is tempted to salvage this historical construct by recasting its metaphysical-historiological schema in heuristic terms. However, Adler proceeds from the aesthetic assumption that equal-voiced counterpoint represents the classical zenith of the polyphonic style whereas the interspersion of functionally subordinate (and hence melodically inconsistent) parts is a sign of archaism or mannerist decline. And if this assumption should prove untenable, Adler's proposed history, even if interpreted in heuristic rather than metaphysical terms, would be deprived of conviction and meaning. It would then be possible only to talk of changes in stylistic ideals, instead of stages within an evolutionary process. And once the notion that a style progresses from archaic to classical and eventually to mannerist stages 'in accordance with the laws of organic evolution' (Adler's solution to our problem) is dismissed as a mere metaphor hypostatised into a law of history, then the forces that caused counterpoint with functionally subordinate parts to evolve into a polyphony of equal voices and back again will continue to elude use.

3

At least from the 1920s onwards, if not earlier, music historians have managed to free the term 'baroque' from the stigma of necessarily denoting a period of stylistic decline. The tendency to neutralise the notion of 'classicism' from a normative category to a label for a stylistic period dates from roughly the same time. 'Tendency' is used here as the reinterpretation has not been entirely successful: it is still hard for us to place Pleyel or Kozeluch unflinchingly under the rubric 'classical'. Informal scholarly parlance – whose conventions reveal the current state of mind in a discipline – allows Pleyel to be called a 'composer of the classical period' but not a 'classical composer'.

However, eliminating the normative connotations of stylistic categories has not left the organism model of the history of style unscathed. If, in Adler's words, the 'intermediate period' forms the 'principal basis of comparison' in style criticism, then this line of criticism hinges unmistakably on a notion of 'classical' as something fully developed and paradigmatic. Consequently, reducing the notion of 'classical' to a descriptive category will likewise affect the organism model, in which the middle stage is invariably the outstanding one. (Strangely enough, not even those epochs that venerated the old felt that a style culminated in its late stages.)

Once the ties between this biological metaphor or analogy and the regulative notion of classicism as being the evolutionary highpoint of a style are loosened, however, all efforts to understand a musical style or complex of stylistic features 'from within' as a unity, and to distinguish it clearly from adjacent styles, tend automatically, one might even say ineluctably, to produce edifices of antithetical concepts shored up by philosophical platitudes – the discussions of 'classical' versus 'romantic' spring immediately to mind. And once we yield to the temptations of argument by anti-thesis it becomes wellnigh impossible to portray a transition, a change of style, that has come about gradually rather than all of a piece: 'qualitative leaps' can be used, as it were, to 'calibrate' the continuity; but far from breaking it they presuppose its existence.

This is not to say that historians of style would dispute the exist-ence of evolutionary gradualism. But this gradualism can scarcely be put into words as long as the terms 'baroque', 'classical' and 'romantic' are understood to mean complexes of features linked together by virtue of a central idea, or aggregate of ideas, that remains unchanged throughout the historical vicissitudes of an age – i.e. as long as historians humble themselves to this method and search for affinities between the beginning and the end of class-icism that are stronger than the similarities between the end of classicism and the beginning of romanticism. Juxtaposing blocks is bad historiography; and it seems as though the historian of style is left facing an awkward dilemma: either he accepts the dubious metaphysics of the organism model and its attendant normative implications, or he chooses to describe the styles of epochs in isola-tion – which is tantamount to dispensing with history altogether.

4

Stylistic history was established early in this century in opposition to the antiquarian's practice of accumulating mountains of undiges-ted facts, and against the principle – derived from the somewhat faded aesthetic of expression – of explaining works by recourse to the biographies of their composers. (It was thought that by imitat-ing the principle of causality – an approach that soon degenerated into caricature – music history would achieve the level of the natural sciences.) In contrast to the positivists, historians of style sought nothing less than a solution to a problem that has constantly challenged scholarly endeavours in the arts: how to write a history of art that is a true history and not a loose amalgam of analyses of works, a history whose subject matter is indeed art and not biogra-phical or social contingencies – a history, in other words, with histo-riographical principles rooted in art itself. Style – in the sense of a distinctive physiognomy produced 'from within' and not, as in the artistic theories of the eighteenth century, a sort of interchangeable orthography – was understood by art historians who wanted to reconcile their aesthetic sensibilities with the demands of historiography to mean, on the one hand, the quintessence of that which makes of something a work of art and, on the other, a sort of numinous entity that changes with the times. Style criticism was supposed to bring together and unite the historical and artistic sides of art; its objective was to mediate between aesthetics and history without doing violence to either. Yet somehow this goal inadvertently dropped out of sight somewhere along the road to its attainment. For as we proceed beyond examining the style of individual works – which means, *ipso facto*, describing their nature as art – and beyond examining the style of individual artists – which, by dint of the originality aesthetic (whereby the artificial and expressive sides of art are equated), likewise converges in the study of works as art – to examine the style of an age or a nation, a concomitant transformation takes place in the musical creation. From being a work of art, or what Ludwig Tieck called a 'world separate unto itself', it is now reduced to mere evidence for ideas, processes or structures lying primarily outside the realm of art, i.e. it becomes no more than a document on the spiritual or social constitution of the age or nation under study. The gulf that separates aesthetics and history is recapitulated within the concept of style itself as a rift in meaning between style as applied to works or composers and style as applied to ages or nations. The individuality of the composer is an essential element in artistic character, originality being one of the defining criteria of art. Yet it can hardly be said of the spirit of an age or nation that it determines the nature of art as art rather than as documentary evidence. We might conceivably maintain this point if we shared the view held by Hegel, and subsequently by the Marxists, that expressive content constitutes the basic substance of art; but this would be to ignore the discovery of more recent aesthetics that it is technical 'form' that determines expressive 'content' rather than the reverse.

2

The significance of art: historical or aesthetic?

In an appendix to his extraordinarily widely read textbook, *A History of Western Music*, Donald Jay Grout offers a 'Chronology' designed 'to provide a background for the history of music, and to enable the reader to see the individual works and composers in relation to their times' (p. 699). Thus, for instance, the year 1843 is represented by *The Flying Dutchman*, Donizetti's *Don Pasquale* and Kierkegaard's *Fear and Trembling*, 1845 by *Les préludes*, *Tannhäuser* and Dumas' *Count of Monte Cristo*, 1852 by *Uncle Tom's Cabin* and Louis Napoléon's *coup d'état*, 1853 by *La traviata* and the Crimean War. However, it is unclear exactly what the reader is meant to conclude. Is there a subtle analogy between Wagner's opera and Kierkegaard's book? Or on the contrary, might it be that events which are extrinsically contemporaneous are, intrinsically, anything but contemporaneous, a conclusion made grotesquely and abundantly clear precisely when we use chronological tables in an attempt to illustrate the *Zeitgeist* that supposedly pervades all spheres of life at a given time? Does music mirror the reality surrounding a composer, or does it propose an alternative reality? Does it have common roots with political events and philosophical ideas; or is music written simply because music has always been written and not, or only incidentally, because a composer is seeking to respond with music to the world he lives in?

The fundamental problem facing the music historiologist is the relation between art and history. This problem will not be solved by adhering to aesthetic or historiographical dogma, whether it be the assumption that art is revealed in its true nature only when separate, self-contained works are contemplated in isolation, or the premise that history consists entirely of causes and effects, ends and means, in endless concatenation. Music history, being the history of an art form, seems doomed to failure: on the one side it is flanked by the dictates of 'aesthetic autonomy', on the other by a theory of history that clings to the concept of 'continuity'. Music history fails either as *history* by being a collection of structural

19

analyses of separate works, or as a history of *art* by reverting from musical works to occurrences in social or intellectual history cobbled together in order to impart cohesion to an historical narrative.

Yet the formalist notion of art that originated in the nineteenth century and owes its present appeal to the hermeticism of our times is not the only one available to an historian who wants to champion history against its philosophically *au fait* detractors. Nor does the opposition of 'functional determinism' and 'aesthetic autonomy' – which has recently kindled a rancorous and not always disinterested polemical debate – provide a theory of art which is sound enough to support a theory of music history. Even making liberal allowances for simplification – within reasonable bounds, of course – we still have to distinguish at least five different approaches to the theory of art, each with its own consequences for the writing of history; and these consequences have to be examined in turn before any pronouncements can be made as to the relationship between the historical and aesthetic dimensions of art.

History and aesthetics exist in a reciprocal relation to one another. The aesthetic premises that might sustain the writing of music history are themselves historical (it would be senselessly dogmatic to ossify them into timeless norms). With some leeway in chronology and some stretching of fact it can safely be said that art theory was based in the sixteenth and seventeenth centuries on the relationship of compositional techniques to social function; in the seventeenth and eighteenth centuries on the 'affections', i.e. the 'objects' represented in music; in the eighteenth and nineteenth centuries on the personalities of individual composers; in the nineteenth and twentieth centuries on the structure of self-contained works; and in the course of the last twenty years on an increasing tendency to view works as documents.[1]

The 'functional' theory of art of the seventeenth century was by and large a theory of musical genres. These were seen to consist of social ends to be met and the musical means held to be appropriate to those ends, both elements standing in fixed correlations governed by norms. When Christoph Bernhard differentiated the repertories of musico-rhetorical figures suitable to church, chamber and theatre music he was in fact claiming, in terms of art theory, that musical means have less to do with the historical stages they

---

[1] 'Even present-day art is being viewed increasingly with an instantaneous historical and critical detachment as a form of document.' (Werckmeister, *Ideologie und Kunst bei Marx*, p. 33.)

represent than with the practical ends they serve. Nor should we judge the association of the *prima prattica* with church music and the *seconda prattica* with theatre music anachronistically: church music was not written with historical detachment as a stylised form of 'early music'; rather, a style appropriate to the liturgy had long since arisen, and its age was taken to be a mark of distinction, a seal of its verity. Monteverdi justified the *seconda prattica* not by calling it progressive but by explaining and praising it as the restoration of an even older verity – the music of the Ancients.

The second paradigm of music aesthetics, the 'doctrine of the affections' found in the seventeenth and eighteenth centuries, is a theory not so much of expression as of objective representation. According to this theory a composer, in his music, conveys the extent of his insights into the nature of a particular human emotion. We understand works of music not by identifying with the emotional workings of the composer's mind so much as by re-creating, in the act of listening, objective truths that the composer has formulated in musical terms – and the representation of emotions is no less an imitation of nature than is naturalistic 'tone painting'. The question of how it is possible to grasp other minds as documented in music did not arise until the mid eighteenth century: understanding music simply meant reaching agreement on its objective contents.

In contrast, the aesthetic of 'expression' that arose during the age of sensibility and *Sturm und Drang* treated the composer as a 'subject' voicing his own thoughts, and hence as the primary 'object' of the process of understanding music. It was no longer the material represented – whether an emotion or the meaning of a text – that formed the decisive aesthetic factor, but the manner of representation and the degree of insight it afforded into the personality of the composer. Style became an expression of the personality 'behind the work', not simply a type of phraseology that a composer could master only to discard it in exchange for another whenever subject or circumstance demanded. This is not to say that concentration on the composer had to degenerate into mere curiosity for biographical detail or anecdote – although this was often enough the case in the nineteenth century: the 'personality' one was meant to empathise with was the 'intelligible ego' of elementary empiricist philosophy, i.e. the composer was taken to be the principal aesthetic arbiter not on the basis of his personal identity but as an artistic persona. Yet this did not alter the fact that the aesthetic substance of a work was to be sought in an individual personality: the 'poetic' element that determines music's nature as art was inseparable from the recognisability of a personality behind the work. In the aesthetic of expression the artistic side of music was by no means incompatible with its documentary character, i.e. the view that a musical work is also a piece of evidence about an individual. On the contrary, the documentary and aesthetic aspects interlocked.

There have been various motives for the polemical tirades directed in our century against the glorification of the composer. For one, they imply that much has changed in the matter at hand, i.e. in the relation of the composer to his work: Stravinsky's distrust of Beethoven and Wagner derived in no small measure from an aversion to the romantic aesthetic of the composer. To put it bluntly, our century regards the composer as a function of his work and not *vice versa*. This new historical development brings with it a corresponding change of intellectual outlook in the methods of interpreting history: the relation of Beethoven or Wagner to their respective oeuvres is not construed now as it was a century ago. (Did *Tristan* have its origins in Wagner's love for Mathilde Wesendonck or was it the other way around, as Paul Bekker suggested?) Yet the problems of determining 'how it really was' stand little chance of being resolved, for the simple reason that it is impossible to reconstruct a 'genuine' psychological state independent of the form that was impressed on the minds of the participating historical agents by the aesthetic notions of their age. If ideas do reflect reality, the reverse is no less true.

The crucial point here is that different aesthetic precepts are at work. The profound difference between nineteenth- and twentieth-century thought on this matter lies not in the conclusion that biographical factors exercise a slighter influence on art than was imagined in the nineteenth century, but rather in the value-judgment that this influence has no aesthetic significance, i.e. plays no part in determining the nature of music as art. The notion that a work of art represents a document about its creator was not so much called into question as summarily dismissed on the grounds of being inimical to art. Even as early as Eduard Hanslick's polemical attack on the 'worm-eaten aesthetic of sentiment' the point was not, as is often believed, that there is no psychological truth to this aesthetic but that it is irrelevant to art.

Thus formalism, or structuralism, was established as the predominant aesthetic of the twentieth century – though it, too, had its detractors. It distinguished between works, which focus largely on themselves, and documents, which refer to something outside themselves, with the true object of musical perception being no longer the composer 'behind' the work but the work itself, a self-contained functional complex variously made up of elements of technical 'form' and expressive 'content'. Sympathetic identification with an individual personality gave way to structural analysis of a musical creation.[2]

Now, in its turn, the meaning and *raison d'être* of this twentieth-century aesthetic of the isolated, self-contained work of art are themselves endangered. Just when it seemed that the 'biography-in-notes' view of works had been done away with once and for all, the documentary aspect of works was rescued from its position in the wings of aesthetics and put stage centre – although this time from a different direction. Ever since World War II there has been a general tendency to listen to music with less interest in the works themselves than in the trends they represent. In extreme cases works collapse to mere sources of information on the latest developments in the compositional techniques they employ. They are perceived less in aesthetic terms, as self-contained creations, than as documentary evidence on an historical process taking place by means of and through them. Contemplation – selfless and dispassionate immersion in the verities of music – has been sacrificed to a mere desire to keep abreast, a position adopted by a few devotees who have mastered the trick of viewing the present, and their own existence in the present, with the detachment of the historian.

The foregoing rough summary of the relations between the different precepts of art theory gives an inadequate picture of how complicated the actual history of these relations has been. To be sure, in succeeding ages the theory of genres was superseded by the doctrine of the affections, the doctrine of the affections by the aesthetic of expression, and this in turn by structuralism, as the dominant view in art theory. Yet the old survived, however peripherally, alongside the new; and the fact that one view 'predominated' – i.e. was accepted by that group of persons whom a consensus of social opinion deemed qualified to pronounce judgment – does not always imply that it was more widely held than another.

---

[2] 'Structure', as defined by aesthetic structuralism, also encompasses expressive elements without at the same time offending the principles of what is unhappily termed 'formalism'. The point is that a work should be viewed 'in its own terms' rather than 'from without'.

Now if, as we have seen, the pattern of aesthetic postulates is less the end result of historical inquiry than an 'ideal type' from which historical inquiry may proceed, it follows that we have even less right to expect these postulates to fall neatly into line with the assumptions of historiography. The rejection of history is a possible, even tantalising, but by no means necessary consequence of structuralism; and a belief in the aesthetic of expression has not prevented a number of historians from writing histories of nineteenth-century music largely along the lines of musical genres, just as though it was the relationship of social function to compositional technique, as crystallised into generic norms, that makes up the real substance of music, rather than the 'poetic' expression of individuality.

Furthermore music historians, like their political counterparts, incline toward eclecticism in their methodology. This is clearly a questionable approach by the standards of philosophy, but not necessarily so as far as the writing of history is concerned. Monographs on composers, structural analyses of fragmentary works, brief histories of various genres, and picturesque extracts from cultural, intellectual or social histories – all are jumbled together with no apparent regard for what, precisely, the object is whose history is being described. There is, of course, no denying that all the facts under discussion have something to do with 'music' in a vague sense; but this scarcely serves to answer our question.

If we nevertheless persevere and attempt to outline a few connections between the precepts of aesthetics and the methods of historiography, we discover that we are dealing with ideal parallels deriving from the logic of these disciplines rather than with real ones actually put to use in the daily business of writing music history.

If it is carried to extremes, the structuralist thesis – that the essence of art lies exclusively in the isolated, self-contained work – amounts to a wholesale rejection of written history; and in all likelihood the tendency of music historians in recent decades to delegate the task of writing large-scale, comprehensive histories to journalists stems not merely from the increasing specialisation of their discipline and their resultant dread of being proved partly incompetent, but also from aesthetic beliefs that make the writing of history a precarious undertaking. For if we consider viewing pieces of music as links in a chain to be inimical to art, an infringement of their aesthetic character, then one sole form of historical presentation remains – which is, strictly speaking, no form at all:

assembling collections of monographs, which can then be re-arranged depending upon which aspect of one we wish to illuminate by its proximity to another. Nor is there even anything to prevent us from dispensing with chronological order altogether if it serves to bring relations supposedly discovered in this imaginary museum of art into sharper focus. Hence the process of 'isolation' that typifies structuralist aesthetics does not mean that the analyst no longer makes connections; it merely means that historical and chronological connections are not the only valid and fundamental ones, and that our interest has been rechannelled from the connections themselves to the works they connect.

A further consequence of this same aesthetic assumption would be a form of history that abandons all hope of reconciliation, as it were, and presupposes a radical distinction between historical and aesthetic significance. Histories of this sort would proceed from the notion (never actually put in such strong terms) that music is 'historical', or amenable to historiographical scrutiny, in inverse proportion to the extent that it qualifies as art. In this view, once art has attained the status of being classical it is elevated beyond the reaches of history and the faculties of historical perception; and by the same token, a work seems to bear an aesthetic stigma if it is possible to make salient points of an historical nature about it.[3]

At the opposite pole to the belief that writing art history is a self-contradictory enterprise, possible only as a history of those aspects of art which are not art at all, stands the nineteenth-century vogue for relating composers and works by registering their mutual interfluence. To avoid the dangers of descending into self-parody this method is seldom applied in undiluted form; instead it is usually interspersed with biographical sketches, observations on the structure of works, and various cultural 'scenes from yesteryear'. Yet this does not alter the fact that it is influences which form the underlying pattern that turns sequences of facts into coherent narrative. Writing music history as though its essence consisted of the effects composers have on one another was the result of a collision between the romantic aesthetic, which located the artistic and 'poetic' dimensions of music in the personality of the

[3] Two different notions of 'historicality' are at work here, the one claiming that to link works of art in historical sequences is to transgress against the nature of art, the other opposing the aesthetic 'presence' of a work to its 'history', meaning something situated in the past and hence dead to the aesthetic faculty. This distinction complicates but does not fatally weaken the position described above.

composer as expressed in music, and historiographical positivism, which broke up musical works into isolated elements in order to arrive at facts that were not only tangible but also fell conveniently into historical sequence. There is, of course, a contradiction between dissecting a work into sub-elements and the aesthetic hypothesis that an indivisible personality – the composer's – determines the nature of music as art; and no doubt this contradiction did not pass unnoticed. Yet it was rendered harmless by being made a feature of the very subject under discussion: this merely methodological distinction between aesthetic 'being' and historical 'becoming', i.e. between contemplation and empirical inquiry, was taken to be a metaphysical dichotomy.

One variant of positivism is the biographical method. This method proceeds from the assumption that we cannot understand a piece of music without first having studied the life of its composer, which it was meant to express in musical form. The search for biographical motives resembles the search for influences which composers have exercised on one another in that both follow from a conflation of the romantic aesthetic of expression and an urge to locate tangible facts as a sort of surety for the scientific quality of music history. By nineteenth-century criteria the biographical method was viable on three grounds: it could be justified in terms of the reigning aesthetic doctrine of the day; it fulfilled the condition that history follow the model of the natural sciences and proceed along strictly empirical lines; and it could pose as self-contained narrative history, with the continuity of a composer's life lending a semblance of continuity to his musical output. The empirical reliability of this procedure, however, went hand in hand with a certain coarsening of the corresponding aesthetic. As the drive toward tangible facts gained supremacy, the personality of the composer, which functioned in aesthetic perception as music's subjective agency, tended to sink from the sublimities of the 'intelligible ego' to the ridiculousness of the merely empirical one. The distinction between the 'intrinsic' biography as evidenced in a composer's musical creations and the 'extrinsic' one revealed in records and documents became progressively weaker. Biographers were faced with the dilemma of sacrificing aesthetic insight for empirical fact or *vice versa* – a dilemma which manifested itself in a dispute between the advocates of idealistic as opposed to realistic biography, the former being scorned as romantic fabricators and the latter as estranged from art.

In our century biography, along with the aesthetic of expression, gradually fell into a decline, its terrain abandoned by scholarship to make way for the mass media. Its legacy fell to social history and the history of reception. Here the method derives from the claim that if we are to understand music historically we must regard it in terms of its social function, i.e. as a process that comprises not only the texts of works but their performance and reception as well. In this view it is not music *per se* (text and work) that has history; rather, history is the property only of society, which includes music among its vital processes.

Adherents of the socio-historical school have been tireless in their campaign against the autonomy principle, but their arguments generally fall short of the mark. To begin with, it is quite defensible in methodological terms for us to isolate an object so long as we do not question the reality of the connections from which it has been extracted. (It is a cheap rhetorical trick to talk about 'false abstractions' without at the same time pointing out – in addition to the indubitable fact that they are abstract – precisely why they happen to be false.) We can always leave the social context of musical works out of consideration without belittling its importance; doing so only means that we consider social context irrelevant to the particular end we have in view, i.e. understanding those inner workings of a piece of music that make it art.

Secondly, the underlying premise of this method – that music should be restored to the social processes that pertained at the time of its origin – makes it virtually impossible to write history in a form that could bear comparison with music histories centred on works. Once we cease merely criticising the autonomy principle and try to implement a counter-programme, the socio-historical approach proves to be fatally handicapped by the paucity and uniformity of the documents available to the history of reception. The concreteness claimed for this method pales into insignificance.

Thirdly, it would appear that the quarrel over the autonomy principle causes two virtually irreconcilable trends to be flung together: the vogue for viewing works solely as sources of information on the evolutionary stage they represent, and the tendency to divert attention from the works themselves onto the surrounding social fabric of which they form a part. The documentary and socio-historical approaches have only one feature in common, namely the negative feature that both totally reject aesthetic immersion in musical works as self-sustaining entities. For the rest, the documentary approach stands above all distinctions between functionality and autonomy: after all, the information it seeks can be concerned as easily with social contexts as with musical technique.

Lastly, aesthetic autonomy is not merely a methodological principle which an historian is free to take or leave, but an historical fact that he has to accept. The workings of the aesthetic faculty are not simply reflex reactions to something taking place within the music; they determine actual musical facts, and the historian who looks for these facts in the acoustical substrate runs the risk of being accused of unpardonable aesthetic naivety. True, artificial music has, since the eighteenth century, been regarded as a text with absolute authority over the listener; but it is equally true that in the nineteenth century, when music was 'autonomised', many works were included that had originally been conceived in terms of function. Historians who emphasise reception as a continuing process – rather than yield to the historiological prejudice that only the reception a work is given at its time of origin counts – should be the last to ignore this transformation of practical music into autonomous works. Consider, for example, the 'Bach renaissance', one of the most noteworthy events of nineteenth-century music. Here works that had originally been conceived in answer to external purposes became open to appreciation (and indeed were appreciated) as *exempla classica* of self-contained musical structures. The idea of absolute music was formed, paradoxically, on the basis of works that first had to be reconstrued before they could even suit this category, a category whose full significance was, in turn, revealed to the nineteenth century only by these very works.

A music historian who deliberately turns a blind eye to the discoveries of art theory in our century so as not to jeopardise the narrative structure of history will forever be plagued by a nagging conscience, his aesthetic misgivings repressed or dulled but never resolved. It is, of course, insufficient to piece together analytical remarks on art works like so many stones in a mosaic and to call the resulting view of the past 'history'; but it is equally inappropriate to resort to cultural, intellectual or social history, which may well link facts into historical narrative but only at the exorbitant price of reducing works of art to their documentary value.

Nevertheless the thought suggests itself that it must be possible to reconcile the autonomy aesthetic with a sense of history, to do justice at one stroke to both the historical and the aesthetic dimensions of musical works without sacrificing either coherence of presentation or the strong concept of art – a concept that has been threatened but, for the moment, not seriously undermined by attempts in recent decades to elevate the documentary view from an extrinsic approach based on cultural history to an intrinsic, aesthetic one rooted in immediate musical experience. Yet it is unlikely that this reconciliation will ever take place unless an interpretation arises that allows us to see the place of an individual work in history by revealing the history contained within the work itself. Art history receives its vindication only to the extent that the historian has read the historical nature of works from their internal constitution; otherwise it remains an *ad hoc* arrangement imposed upon art and art works from the outside.

A perfect example of just such a reconciliation is offered by the Russian formalist theory of literature for the simple reason that its underlying aesthetic criterion – the novelty or individuality of the artistic devices employed – is at the same time an historical element enabling the construction of continuous historical sequences. Admittedly, one might question whether the concept of 'innovation', which is meant to be an alternative to casual, mundane, stereotyped perception, does sufficient justice to both aesthetic and historical reality. Yet, however seriously this objection must be considered, it should not overshadow the fact that, objectively speaking, formalism has lit upon at least part of the truth and we would be ill-advised to part with it. Nor should we overlook the fact that formalism, being a fusion of aesthetic and historiographical approaches, is exemplary in point of methodology.

'Art', writes Theodor W. Adorno in his *Aesthetische Theorie*, 'is historical solely on the basis of separate and individual works considered on their own merits, and not by virtue of their external relationships, let alone the influence they supposedly exercised on each other' (p. 263). Yet when we compare the historiographical axiom implicit in this proposition with Adorno's actual writings on the philosophy of history (in his *Philosophie der neuen Musik* he illustrated his thesis of the historical movement of musical material by using abstract categories such as 'chord', 'dissonance' and 'counterpoint' rather than analyses of works), then the contradiction becomes only too obvious, and no amount of assurance that these categories derive from analyses will remove it. This is not a case of an incidental shortcoming, or of failure on the part of the author, but of a conflict of principles that seems practically insoluble: how to reach agreement on a permissible amount of abstraction that will keep a music history from suffocating in details without being so far removed from individual works as to obliterate all sense of the particular, the unreduplicatable and individual, so that nothing survives of the intended history of composition but a history of musical techniques.

The dialectical argument that Adorno devised in his *Philosophie der neuen Musik* (1958, pp. 53–5) to demonstrate the historical origins of dodecaphonic technique typifies the hazards of carrying abstraction too far:

Traditional music had to make do with an extremely limited number of combinations of notes, especially in regard to vertical combinations. It had to be content to find the Specific by means of configurations of the General – configurations which, paradoxically, make the General appear identical with the Unique . . . By comparison, chords nowadays are tailor-made for the particular requirements of each separate occurrence. There are no longer any *convenus* to prevent the composer from applying the sound that he needs at a given moment and this moment only . . . Hand in hand with this liberation of the material came increasingly greater possibilities of bringing the material under technical control.

The 'technical control' that Adorno has in mind apparently consists of the perfect dovetailing of chords within the functional contexts of the individual works in which they appear. However, once the 'emancipation of dissonance' had freed chords from the burden of having to resolve, or even form progressions, it could no longer be taken for granted that they would form a connected tissue rather than merely standing unrelated alongside one another; and it was left to each individual work to demonstrate afresh that this was in fact the case. The demise of the *convenus* or 'agreements' mentioned by Adorno prevents general observations from being made on the functioning of chords, on whether they at all continue to fulfil the function of endowing a work with coherence.

The various dimensions of Western tonal music – melody, harmony, counterpoint, form and orchestration – have in the main evolved independently of each other with no preconceived plan. In this sense they have evolved 'indigenously'. Even in those cases in which one of these dimensions became a function of another – as for instance in the romantic period, when melody become a function of harmony – the one did not, strictly speaking, emerge from the other. On the contrary, there was a process of mutual adaptation and assimilation.

Quite apart from the fact that only in a perverse sort of utopia would one 'plan' to deprive music of its 'indigenousness', this line of argument suffers from an arbitrary placing of emphasis. Those dissonances whose emancipation led to the emergence of twelve-note music had always, in traditional music, been determined not only by harmony but by melody as well (witness the rules of preparation and resolution) and by metre (witness the varying treatment

of dissonance depending on its position within the bar). And deciding whether the relation between melody and harmony in the nineteenth century was one of 'mutual adaptation' or 'dialectical reconciliation' rests finally on a terminological preference that cannot be
substantiated or refuted objectively by any known criteria.

The productive forces of music, particularly after Beethoven, developed
with a blindness that led to discrepancies. Whenever in the course of
history one area of the material was developed in isolation, others
invariably remained backward, giving the lie to the progressive features by
undermining the unity of the work . . . These discrepancies, however, are
not simply confined to details of technique; they become historical forces
at work within the whole. For the further the separate areas of the material
evolve, or even at times fuse, as did harmony and timbre during
romanticism, the more clearly does the idea raise its head that these discrepancies can be eliminated by means of a rational, thorough organisation
of the music material in its entirety . . . In Schoenberg's music, the dimensions have not only all evolved to the same degree; they have emerged
from each other mutually and reciprocally to the extent that they have
converged.

Adorno, for the purposes of his argument, has transformed the
premise (derived from Schoenberg) that all areas of the material of
music must be at an equivalent stage of development if inconsistency is to be avoided into an 'historical force'; and indeed one of
the basic patterns of his philosophy of history is to reconstrue aesthetic norms into historical trends to form a basis for a pre-history
of the twelve-note technique. However, it is not only the confusion
of an abstract postulate with a concrete trend that is at question
here, but also the central premise of Adorno's train of thought.
Analysis can scarcely be called upon to verify the claim that an
unequal evolution of material results in aesthetic and compositional flaws. This claim bears more resemblance to an historical-
philosophical decree than to the outcome of a considered and
impartial interpretation of individual pieces. Not only that; it is
never exactly clear what is meant by the alleged 'backwardness' of
Wagner's or Brahms's rhythm. It would, of course, be absurd to
assess the rhythm of *Tristan* by the standards of, say, *The Rite of
Spring*; but it would be equally futile to attempt to demonstrate a
discrepancy between rhythm and harmony within *Tristan* itself. On
the other hand, it is patent nonsense to maintain of Schoenberg's
twelve-note works that 'the dimensions have all evolved to the
same degree', for the vertical dimension obviously 'lags behind' the
horizontal. Adorno's argument is abstract in the negative sense. Its

underlying aesthetic premises, the historical conclusion it aspires to prove and the historiological paths it follows – all are equally fallible.

It would thus seem that attempts to reconcile aesthetics and history without resorting to devious methodology, and to settle upon a level of abstraction that would permit the writing of lucid history without at the same time violating the aesthetic nature of works of music by reducing them to mere illustrations of techniques or ideas – attempts, in other words, to bridge the gap between the history inherent in a work by reason of its artistic nature and the course charted by works in history – are all doomed to failure by their very nature. A counter-proposal exists in the form of a 'dual language' theory, according to which aesthetics and history must be viewed as separate languages treating the same object but incapable of being translated into one another. While the aspects of the subject matter revealed by the respective terminologies do complement each other, they can never be considered valid at one and the same time: anyone who adopts the aesthetic standpoint will have to abandon the historical one and *vice versa*.

Attractive as it is, the 'dual language' thesis has its fatal flaw. It overlooks the fact that it is nevertheless possible, without self-contradiction, to subsume historical knowledge into aesthetic perception, and by the same token to take aesthetic experiences as points of departure for historical investigations. A history of the nineteenth-century symphony that did not build upon an interpretation of the 'immanence' of the Eroica would lack all sense of direction. Of course one offends against the aesthetic *raison d'être* of art works by analysing them as documents in a social, intellectual or technical history of music; but this does not imply that one must refrain from considering the results of historical studies of this sort when interpreting the aesthetic essence of those works. Aesthetic and documentary observations, while motivated by opposing interests, are not necessarily based on different and mutually exclusive groups of facts: just which sorts of facts are to be used in an historical or an 'immanent' interpretation is not determined *a priori* but must be decided upon in each individual case. The historian who feels that the 'immanent' or 'indwelling' interpretation is indispensable in the light of the aesthetic nature of art is in no way bound to disregard 'external' documents; he merely stands by his belief that it is the 'intrinsic', functional coherence of a work that serves as the final arbiter in deciding which facts do or do not belong to the matter at hand. Distinguishing between internal, aesthetic observations and external, documentary ones is a matter of choosing one's main areas of interest and principles of selection, not of deciding which sorts of facts are relevant or how to go about obtaining them.

3

What is a fact of music history?

What a fact of music history is seems to need no explanation. Works of music and performances of them, the matters surrounding the lives of the composers who wrote them, the structures of the institutions for which they were intended, even the aesthetic ideas of the age and the social strata that sustain musical genres – none of these has ever been denied a place among the facts which go to make up a piece of music history. Nor do music historians feel specially upset to learn that the range of facts in music history is by nature boundless. It obviously depends on how the question is formulated as to whether any given state of affairs forms, or does not form, a fact of music history, one that figures in the picture of music history given in the preceding chapter. However this may be, the assurance that works, composers, institutions and ideas at all events form a central core of the facts of music history offers a firm support, even in the face of open boundaries.

Yet even the most casual attempt to learn how musical and music-historical facts are related and in what sense a musical fact can be regarded at all as an historical one leads us quickly along tortuous byways, and the difficulties that entangle us are by no means simply phantoms conjured up by unnecessary and, for the historian, irrelevant speculations. The present-day aesthetic experience of a work written a century and a half ago is obviously not the same thing as the acquisition of a music-historical fact, no matter whether the aesthetic perception takes due account of the intervening time-lag. What does it mean, then, to say that a work represents a music-historical fact? Where is the historical aspect to be found: in the composer's intention, which the historian, in his faltering manner, seeks to reconstruct; in the musical structure, which he analyses according to the criteria of the history of forms and genres; or in the consciousness of the original public for whom the work became an 'event' – a consciousness which, though not accessible as an individual element, nevertheless manifests some determinable general traits characteristic of an age, a generation and a stratum of society?

It is one of the basic tenets of the historical sciences that documents – the data at an historian's disposal – must be distinguished from the facts which he reconstructs from these data: not the source itself, but the process it refers to, represents an historical fact, a component part of an historical narrative. The elementary nature of this tenet does not, indeed, prevent even historians from overstepping or losing sight of it. Hence a 'documentary biography', for instance, insofar as it makes the reader feel closer to historical reality than is ever possible in accounts by historians, is seen to be a thoroughly ambivalent genre when it is measured against the criteria of historical method. Doubtless the local colour which exudes from the documents is seductive. But a document, strictly speaking, does not reveal 'the way it really was', but rather only what its author thought of an event. And reading documents as they should be read calls for a number of precautionary measures which, though second nature to an historian, the average reader of a documentary biography will in all probability not light upon. One cannot even exclude the possibility that, in the minds of its readers, the documentary biography has assumed the function formerly held by the faded genre of the historical romance.

Reading documents in a way that reflects history involves being caught up in a sort of 'source-critical circle' in which knowledge of the persons, things and events spoken of is constantly measured against what is known about the author himself: his reliability and inclinations, the purpose the document was meant to fulfil and the formal tradition it is dependent upon. What Charles Burney has to say about C. P. E. Bach is a source not only on Bach but on Burney as well; and the more precise the text seems in the one direction the more reliably it can be interpreted in the other. Even if the document is of interest solely for the light it sheds on its subject, it is by no means irrelevant to investigate its author, not merely by asking what he saw and heard – and whether he had reasons for not disclosing the truth – but by bearing in mind who he was and what assumptions underlay his thoughts and feelings.

The distinction between datum and fact, easy as it is to demonstrate with documents, seems to fail when applied to the main object of music history – works. 'And what', asks Droysen, 'are we supposed to do with this sort of critical method in a history of literature, or of art, where the desired objective facts lie ready to hand?'[1] In what form, it should be asked, do works of music form 'the desired objective facts' that comprise music history? As musical constructions presented to the aesthetic faculty of the historian, and hence partly determined by subjective elements? As sources such as they are, or as 'authentic texts' puzzled together by source criticism? Or as the composer's intention, to be reconstructed from the text in conjunction with other documents? The concept of a work, seemingly the most stable element of music history, dissolves into a source, an authentic text, a composer's intention and an historian's notion as to the musical significance of the acoustical substrate sketched out by the text or realised according to the guidelines laid down within it.

The distinction between works of music and political events which Droysen is apparently aiming at – between producing and acting, *poiesis* and *praxis* – must on no account be obscured or minimised: the possibility of an aesthetic presence which can be recaptured in later performances distinguishes a work of music fundamentally and profoundly from a political event, which belongs once and for all to the past and only extends into the present by virtue of reports or remnants of it. Yet we must not overlook the fact that a work of music, brought to our aesthetic consciousness, is precisely *not* perceived as an historical fact (despite an awareness of history which colours our aesthetic perceptions). And if one tries to clarify the logical status of a remnant from the musical past, as conceived in terms of history, one feels drawn willy-nilly to the assumption that the sources of musical works are just as much 'remnants' as are treaties, letters or architectural ruins – relics that do not represent the desired historical facts as such but are simply the givens from which historical facts in the true sense have to be deduced.

The historian must resist the deeply ingrained habit of thinking that the word 'fact' refers to something tangible since, to put it bluntly, an historical fact is nothing more than an hypothesis. The accounts and relics that serve as the historian's starting point form the data which have survived into the present and which the historian seeks to explain by making an assumption about past events. And it is these conceptualised events, and not the given materials, that represent the historical facts he seeks.

It cannot be denied that the distinction between data and facts

---

[1] *Historik*, p. 96.

is relative and has hierarchical gradations. In historiology, the theory of the historical sciences, we need not go into the relation between sense data and categorically formed perceptions. The problems of the epistemologist are not those of the historian. Nevertheless, even within history, and music history as well, data can be distinguished from facts on several levels: a particular source is a datum used in deducing the fact 'authentic text'; this authentic text serves in turn as a datum for the fact 'work', in the sense of a functional complex of musical meanings; and the work, for its part, is a datum for the fact 'composer', upon whose originality (meaning an amalgam of novelty and creation *ab origine*, i.e. from a mind of unreduplicatable individuality) the historical nature of the work depends, 'history' being understood to mean a sequence of innovations. Consequently, an historical interpretation is almost invariably an interpretation of other interpretations.

However, the claim that historical facts are, strictly speaking, hypotheses must be qualified so as not to lead to misunderstandings by way of hidden equivocations. On the one hand its objective is the trivial notion that history, by belonging to the past, escapes immediate perception: documents that an historian can hold in his hands do not in themselves constitute the past event but are merely a reflection or relic of it. Yet at the same time, calling facts 'hypotheses', though offensive to untutored ears, also stresses the point that the facts that an historian really desires reside less in visible or audible events themselves than in the motives, ideas and trends that gave rise to them. 'Remnants such as sources are historical material for us only insofar as they provide knowledge of events of bygone times, that is to say, of acts of will which, by their presence and influence in their own time, brought about the things we wish to summon forth again in the form of history' (*ibid.* p. 98).

Seen in this light, the ultimate goal of history is to comprehend or explain past human actions. (The difference between intentional interpretations and causal or functional relations will be taken up later in other contexts.) And however profound the distinction between political and social action and the production of works may be, it little affects the basic structure of historical knowledge: historians still refer to the conscious or unconscious motives that underlie documented events or surviving texts, and are fully convinced on the basis of their experiences with themselves and others that these motives have a claim to reality.[2]

---

[2] Despite the urgent need for a psychology or anthropology of history there have as yet been scarcely any efforts in this direction.

The realisation that historical facts are always based on interpretations need not be disturbing. Strictly speaking, the 'raw facts' sometimes spoken of by historians when they feel harassed and fatigued by the problems of hermeneutics do not exist. We cannot posit the existence of facts without, at the same time, qualifying them by the language we use. For example, the apparently unimpeachable remark that Beethoven's *Missa solemnis* was first performed on 18 April 1824 in St Petersburg is based on a number of concepts that in no way express a bare fact but derive from calendrical, liturgical, political ('St Petersburg') and aesthetic ('first performance') systems without which these concepts would be incomprehensible. The transition to second- or third-level interpretations, e.g. by recourse from sources to texts, from texts to works and from works to the intentions behind them, may well increase still further the sense of uncertainty that nearly always plagues historians, but it does not fundamentally alter the inescapably hypothetical nature of historical facts. The historian's own particular interests will determine which are the 'real' facts he seeks in this hierarchy of data and facts. Granted that comprehending past human action is the ultimate goal of history, the interest of music history attaches mainly to the poetics that underlie a composer's work.

No conflict of principles arises until an historian adopts a theory of art which bypasses the personality of the creator and takes the structure of works as the one and only valid object of any field deserving of being called a science of art. Structuralism of this sort is hostile to history so as to be congenial to art. And according to structuralist criteria, the writing of music history is an impossible venture caught on the horns of an insoluble dilemma: either it fails to take the form of history at all, being nothing more than a jumble of structural analyses of individual works; or, by simply recounting 'extrinsic' conditions and circumstances, it aims wide of its target of being a science of art. What an historian reconstructs as music-historical fact – the composer's thought as part of the past – is of no consequence to rigorous structuralists, who discard both the author's intention and the temporal nature of works of art. Yet as long as a theory of art predominates that binds the artistic nature of music to categories such as 'originality' and 'expressive content', which are rooted in the notion of composers as historical agents, then the writing of music history can still be reconciled with the tenet that the 'object' of history consists in human action without at the same time inviting the criticism that music history is alien to art.

To stress the composer as the vehicle and 'subjective' agency of history is, however, to draw on historical assumptions which are themselves historical and hence subject to change. And these particular assumptions cannot simply be transferred from the classical and romantic periods, where they were taken as matters of course, to earlier or more recent times. It is not at all clear, indeed rather unlikely, that the individuality of the composer provides the best point of departure for a proper understanding of the history of, say, fifteenth-century music, not as recaptured today in musical performance but as it was in its own day. This is not to say that it would be irrelevant and futile to distinguish between 'personal' styles in this music; but a music history that tacitly accepts the originality postulate so as to apply the criteria of novelty and originality in selecting from the vast profusion of surviving musical facts those deemed essential or worthy of consideration would inevitably, if unconsciously, be an anachronism as regards the fifteenth century.

It would thus seem as though the methods of music history derive from premises in art theory that themselves vary with time, with the result that any history of fifteenth-century music which uses facts of a different kind – as opposed to different facts of the same kind – is more likely than not to convey an image of the nineteenth century. Music-historical facts, or at least the essential ones (for, as already mentioned, there are ultimately no limits as to what falls within the scope of music history), are subject to two basic conditions. As *historical* facts they are bound to serve the function of making up historical narrative or descriptions of historical structures; as *musical* facts, however, they are equally dependent upon the prevailing notion of a given age, region or social stratum as to what constitutes music. For music history has not always been primarily the history of works and composers: to claim otherwise we would have to seek refuge in the argument that music history in those ages that lacked an aesthetic of works was not, properly speaking, history at all.

In a similar manner the history of the reception of music, which many historians regard as a viable alternative to the history of composers and works, should be 'historicised' and its proclaimed universality of scope reduced to particularity. This approach, insofar as it aspires to the status of a major rather than a merely peripheral discipline, is based on the aesthetic premise that it is not so much musical works, i.e. texts available for structural analysis or relevant to a particular composer, that constitute the essential musical and

music-historical facts, but rather a complex of functional relationships between a text, its performance, and its reception. Obviously this assumption, if widely accepted, would lead to profound
changes in the aims and methods of music history.

If music is viewed less as a corpus of works than as an event, a
'communicative process', then the main emphasis of musical philo-
logy and the compiling of musical editions no longer falls exclusively on 'authentic' texts, i.e. those reflecting the intentions of the
composer. On the contrary, inauthentic versions, being documents
of particular modes of reception, enjoy equal rights as historical
evidence, particularly if they were widely used in their own time.
Another result of the 'reception' approach is a general shift in the
chronology of music history, with dates of composition giving way
to dates of greatest influence or effect, vague though they may be.
In these terms, the years around the turn of the century would be
noted less for having witnessed the appearance of Mahler's symphonies than for being the high-water mark of Wagner's music
dramas. However, the proposed 'history of events' directed towards real processes instead of abstract texts merges inadvertently
with 'structural history': the manner in which individuals or groups
actually 'receive' music is seldom documented, so the historian of
reception has no alternative but to describe general functional relationships between compositional models, conventional patterns of
perception, aesthetic ideas, ethical norms, and the roles and institutions of society. The aesthetic premise behind the history of reception – the thesis as to what music 'really' is – does not make good
historiographical tender.

Hence the apparent nearness to reality that makes the reception
approach to history so attractive turns out to be in part a deception.
Musical events, unlike authentic texts, cannot be adequately
reconstructed. And insisting that music ultimately resides in the
'communicative process' and not in the 'dead letter' will carry little
or no weight when confronted with the disappointing discovery that
the stereotyped evidence which historians of reception are forced
to resort to from want of documents can hardly vie with the
subtleties attainable by structural analysis of music. Moreover, reception has not always figured to an equal extent and with equal
importance at all times and in all genres in that complex of
phenomena which a given culture chooses to call 'music'. To be
sure, the *raison d'être* of a sixteenth-century German *geselliges
Lied* may have had precious little to do with a composer's intention;
but it is no less a fact that nineteenth-century concert audiences

subordinated themselves without a murmur to the authority of Beethoven. Here the 'ideal' listener sought by historians of reception can be considered as identical with the intention behind the composer's text: deviations were regarded as failure or inadequacy on the listener's part.

Now if, as we have seen, the musical side to music-historical facts is determined by changeable notions as to what constitutes music, it is no less true that for a text to be historical it must appear in a context, i.e. as part of an historical narrative or an account of an historical structure. Bygone events, *res gestae*, become historical facts in the strict sense only as part of an *historia rerum gestarum*. As Droysen put it:

Whatever occurs must first be perceived as part of a coherent process, as a complex of cause and effect, end and means – in short, as a 'fact' – before it can be comprehended and digested; and these features can be perceived differently by different people, and combined with different causes, effects or ends (*ibid*. pp. 133–4).

Facts become historical facts by virtue of the continuity that binds them together.

Hence no-one before Aristotle thought of poetry as having a history; and no-one before, roughly, the middle of our century would have thought to speak of a history of music (*ibid*. p. 138).

No matter that Droysen's dating of the dawn of historical awareness in music is untenable in the light of the historical writings of Burney, Hawkins and Forkel; the main point is his argument, reminiscent of Hegel, that a series of events must be apprehended by the historical faculty before it can figure as history at all.

History is not the past as such, but what the historical faculty is able to make of the past – what the historian pulls in when he casts his net. The structure of this faculty – its capacity to select, measure and classify – leaves its mark on the objects it apprehends. We can never reconstruct the actual sequence of causes between past events. The chains of facts put forth by historians – the context which turns raw source material or 'data' into historical fact in the first place – are by their nature mental constructs.

Historians quite often prefer not to specify the structural frameworks behind their historical narratives. Far from lessening the significance of these frameworks for the writing of history, however, this practice only renders them all the more effective. Suppose, for instance, that in a history of nineteenth-century music we were to mention the destruction of the décor for E. T. A. Hoffmann's *Undine* during the burning of the old Berlin Schauspielhaus in 1817 and to follow this fact immediately and without further comment by referring to the use four years later of Weber's *Freischütz* to inaugurate the new Schauspielhaus. This would suggest a music-historical connection as represented by the destruction and rebuilding of the theatre. And in fact the influence of *Undine* did come to an abrupt end with this catastrophe, and the opera figures in the history of German romantic opera as a 'preliminary stage' en route to *Der Freischütz*, as a tentative experiment whose aesthetic and historical significance was 'sublated' (as the Hegelians would say) into the later and more perfect work. Seen from the perspective of 'romantic opera' – a generic term with no particularly strong foothold in reality – the extrinsic correspondence between these two events lends itself to a narrative music history because it allegorises an intrinsic one.

Without the links supplied by mental constructs any picture of the past would, in Max Weber's words, disintegrate into a 'chaos of "existential judgments" on countless individual perceptions'.[3] Even then it is doubtful whether 'existential judgments' can ever be made without qualifications. Anyone who tries to grasp the essence of history from outside the conceptual systems that make it accessible even while they distort it abandons history for mysticism.

The use of the term 'construct' is meant to make it abundantly clear that no linking of occurrences in the mind of the historian will ever mirror an 'actual' sequence of causes. This does not imply, however, that historians proceed arbitrarily, relying on their fantasy in the manner of novelists – though to look at the many blatantly antithetical constructs which are nevertheless equally well grounded in the sources, one might well sympathise with the sceptic's view that historical facts have nothing more pressing to do than accommodate themselves to mutually exclusive hypotheses. History, if it is to be distinguishable from fiction, must be rooted in source material. Yet it is disturbing to note that, by nature, the amount of source material and the potential number of historical connections it contains are boundless. For a construct, even if vindicated by sufficient data ('sufficiency' being determined among historians by consensus of opinion), is necessarily selective. More-

---

[3] *Gesammelte Aufsätze zur Wissenschaftslehre*, p. 177.

over it is based on concepts that in large part were not present to the minds of the historical agents but were supplied later by the historian. While it is facts, not fancies, that confront the honest historian, these facts have nevertheless been selected on the basis of particular interests, and have risen from the status of mere source material to that of historical fact solely by virtue of a conceptual system of the historian's own making.

Consequently the fact that the structure of history depends upon the language in which the historian discloses it should not be taken in the sceptical sense to mean that the discoveries of historians are nothing more than inventions: history is an empirical science, and as such rests entirely on facts, however much these facts depend for their existence on the categories of human perception. Even structures and sequences are predetermined in the reality conveyed to the historian by his sources, though to be sure they cannot be made explicit except by means of conceptual systems devised by the historian. The fact that they are bound to appear within a particular perspective is the necessary condition for their appearing at all – a condition that an historian can never escape from any more than he can flee his own shadow, without leaving the impression that he is lost in a maze of fictions. Histories written in full knowledge of the nature of history strike a precarious balance between two false extremes – naive objectivism and destructive radical scepticism.

We have seen that facts from the past do not actually become historical facts until they are made part of an historical narrative or a description of an historical structure. It is in this sense that the material of history can be said to be determined by its form. And form also involves mode of presentation, i.e. narrative technique, which cannot be interchanged without altering the coloration of the facts. If, say, a chapter in a history of music were to open with the sentence 'On 19 October 1814 Franz Schubert composed his "Gretchen am Spinnrade"', the meaning of this remark would not simply end with the surface information it conveys. On the contrary, the location of this statement – which may seem harmlessly descriptive but is itself the product of a system of interpretation – expresses a view as to the origins of the romantic lied. No subsequent reference to the writing of a lied by Weber or Spohr is likely to dislodge it from its commanding position. And should it ever happen that a history of nineteenth-century music opened with the remark 'On 20 February 1791 Carl Czerny was born', this would involve less the transmission of a fact than an announcement that a roundabout and tortuous argument was about to begin in *ex post facto* justification of such obviously grotesque placing of emphasis.

The dependence of historical facts on interpretation – the discovery that the facts transmitted by an historian already imply a certain theory – should not, however, blind us to the differences of degree between firmly and less firmly established facts. Strictly speaking there are, of course, no 'raw' facts in history, any more than there are in the natural sciences, whose theoretical foundations are plagued with the problems surrounding 'basis' or 'protocol' statements; but this does not mean that we should capitulate in the face of the competing interpretative systems of history and forego judgments altogether in the mistaken belief that we are caught in a vicious circle, in which the historical facts supposedly required to evaluate incompatible interpretations have themselves resulted from interpretations without which they would not have become historical facts in the first place. There is no doubt that the grossly conflicting portraits of Spontini, Spohr or Mendelssohn given by history are irreconcilable in many respects. And there is little solace to be had in the hope that they have resulted from perspectives which 'in the final analysis' will prove to be complementary: considering that it is precisely in histories of distinction that 'subject' and 'object' are inextricably interwoven, it is more likely to be the case that the divergent views mutually exclude and thwart one another.

Yet histories do have at least a modicum of substance in common, since besides those facts that are highly prone to interpretation there exist others that prove to be virtually immutable (the qualification 'virtually' is unavoidable even for the most firmly established of facts, on the one hand because there are ultimately no limits to the context in which they can appear, on the other because there are no standards for measuring the extent to which a fact has become historical simply by virtue of its context). The relatively invariant facts that make up the framework of history are, however, to the historian who is more than a mere archivist, interesting less for their own sakes than for the function they fulfil in vindicating or refuting competing interpretative systems. To put it bluntly, historical facts have no other reason for being than to substantiate historical narratives or descriptions of historical systems, unless it is to serve the negative purpose of revealing flaws in the opinions of earlier historians.

4

Does music history have a 'subject'?

One reason why history seems to be endangered and at odds with the *Zeitgeist* might be found in the banal fact that it has become difficult to write history without the nagging thought that the past as it really was cannot be recounted in narrative form. Disparagers of traditional history have long suspected that narratives compounded from events emerge less from the structure of the materials concerned than from the historian's sense of form. The 'explanation sketch', as Arthur C. Danto would call it, has its roots in the historian's original intention to proceed by narration, rather than by explication as in the natural sciences. And while the concept of narrative history automatically conjures up the image of an unbroken landscape and a continuous chain of events, it turns out to be fragile and precarious the moment we begin to analyse it instead of merely treating it as one of those timeless truths that tend to dominate our thinking precisely because we never think about them.

What, then, is the cohesive force that makes historical narration possible? The question obviously – or so it would seem – aims at discovering a 'subjective agency' in history that maintains its identity throughout the vicissitudes of change, thereby guaranteeing an unbroken continuity that prevents our picture of the past from disintegrating into unrelated fragments. Until several decades ago the notion of an historical 'subject' – the necessary condition for casting history in narrative form – retained a healthy plausibility, deriving in all likelihood from the biographical model that historians, and music historians among them, drew upon for long stretches even when they were least aware of doing so. The most cursory glance at recent music histories will suffice to show that it is not 'music' as such – i.e. the musical 'event', an amalgam of composition, performance and reception – so much as individual composers that serve as vehicles for the lesser sub-histories that go to make up 'music history'. Even when the historical subject is a musical genre or style rather than a composer, the 'life-history' metaphor that art historians have instinctively turned to ever since Winckelmann and Herder reveals that the evolutionary stages of the genre or style have been made analogous to the ages of the

44

human lifespan in order to give structure and solidity to the historical narrative. References to periods of 'flowering', 'maturity' or
'late decline' are not simply rhetorical ingredients that we can
expunge from histories of style without altering their substance.
On the contrary, this language proves to be an expression of the
historiological framework that, implicitly or explicitly, holds such
histories together.[1]

Even in the field of biography, however, it has proved more
problematical than not to pinpoint this 'subject' that allegedly
forms the backbone of historical narration, for it is not one of
nature's givens but results from a deliberate effort on the subject's
part to represent its own past, mingled with the present, as coherent history. The subject does not simply 'have' a history; it must
produce one, and only in so doing does it become a subject at all.
Hence it bears a circular relation to historical narration. However,
the more endangered the concept of a subject appears in its own
right, the more precarious would it seem to apply it to ideas,
epochs, or even to 'History' as a whole. This would hardly need
mentioning were the habit of taking the narrative structure of biography as the model for written history not so deeply ingrained as
to obviate all need to question how and in what form genres or
styles have a history at all. To nineteenth- and early-twentieth-
century historians the biographical approach seemed all the more
compelling because it represented the mainstay of historical hermeneutics. This approach took as its model the practice of interpreting texts so as to acquire a sympathetic understanding of their
authors, thereby allowing historians to apprehend history 'from
within' rather than merely ordering it chronologically 'from without'. Insofar as the historian (the 'subject' of written history)
chooses to study objects which like himself are also 'subjects'
(though in the strong sense of being historical figures acting in full
awareness of the continuity of their lives), it is entirely appropriate
for him to resort to narrative in writing his history: in Kantian terminology, the transcendental structure of the narrative would
accord with the ontological structure of its object. If, however, we
abandon the biographical model altogether – and it seems less and
less likely that we can salvage it – then narrative history will arouse
the suspicion of being the contrivance of an imaginary subject.

---

[1] Erich Rothacker spoke of an 'organism model' for art histories, and explained its
appearance in terms of the history of ideas without considering its narrative function.

All this leads to the supposition that if continuity in history is to be conveyed at all the historical narrative must have a 'subject' with a consistent and fixed identity – or, put in negative terms, that the notion of continuity stands or falls with that of identity. Yet this supposition is not necessarily valid outside the field of biography from which it was extracted; indeed, the opposite is more likely to be the case. Anyone who wishes to write, say, a history of the motet, a history spanning some eight centuries, would be hard pressed to find a single feature (apart from polyphony) in common between the secular, multiple-text, isorhythmic and partially instrumental motet of the fourteenth century and its sacred, single-text, imitative and purely vocal sixteenth-century counterpart. Nevertheless there undoubtedly exists an historical thread to justify the contention that what has been handed down in this case is, in fact, a musical genre and not a mere technical term. A contrary instance would be the madrigal, whose fourteenth- and sixteenth-century versions have nothing in common but their name. Here the break in tradition that occurred in the fifteenth century makes nonsense of any talk about a continuous history of this genre. It would seem therefore that historical continuity presupposes not so much the identity of an historical vehicle – an identity residing in features which are tangible – as a sense of unbroken succession.[2]

The question naturally arises as to why the functional liturgical music of fourteenth-century England, which was a significant historical forebear of the Netherlands motet, should even today be denied the name 'motet', or similarly why the seventeenth-century sacred concerto should no longer be classified as 'motet' (contemporary practice varied on this point) despite the fact that as regards text and function, if not style, it carried on the sixteenth-century tradition. Clearly there is no little arbitrariness to historians' decisions as to which congeries of features are sufficient to establish the historical continuity of a genre or, conversely, which changes are so far-reaching as to signify the emergence of a new genre despite the fact that some earlier characteristics have been retained. Yet in principle it is quite possible to establish by empirical methods (rather than by normative or dogmatic decree) for a given age just how much importance to attach to continuity or

[2] We need not pursue the possibility of defining identity in such a way as to make it appear vouchsafed by continuity, as this is a philosophical refinement of no consequence to the problems of historiography.

discontinuity in text and function, style and technique, and terminology when deciding whether a genre has survived or died out.
Thus, to continue our example, the separation of the sacred concerto from the seventeenth-century motet is rooted in the assumption, usually tacit, that stylistic and technical considerations (in this
case the transition from imitative polyphony to concertante
monody) take precedence over those involving text or function.
Consequently, the weighting of these criteria should be substantiated and justified in seventeenth-century terms – a difficult but
presumably not impossible task – so as to avoid reflecting the
early-twentieth-century bias towards autonomy in works of art.

Now if, as this would suggest, the continuity of a history is not
always tied to the identity of the subject of an historical narrative
(an identity consisting in the durability of a complex of features),
then we might even go so far as to ask whether continuity is a necessary prerequisite for historical narration at all. Siegfried Kracauer[3]
and Hans Robert Jauss,[4] for instance, have shown that the nineteenth-century historian's notion of continuity was related in
substance to that of contemporary novelists – or, to put it drastically, that Ranke took his narrative technique from Scott – and
conversely that the sense of form and reality at the heart of the
modern novel ever since Proust and Joyce might very well be
influencing the manner in which historians combine their facts and
hypotheses, thereby bringing historians closer to a modern awareness as to what reality actually is and how it can be captured in
language. In other words, granted that the forms and structures of
the novel are vehicles for voicing fragments of reality previously
condemned to silence, it follows that there is no reason why an
historian should adopt a scholarly pose bordering dangerously
close on provincialism and shun modern narrative techniques on
principle, preferring instead to cling to tried and true methods
which, however artless and blandly descriptive they may appear to
the naive reader, are in fact as much beholden to formal artifice as
are modern procedures, the only difference being that their artifices are older. (This is not to say that these older methods are by
nature obsolete, but the possibility of their being so in many cases
should not be discounted.) A modern historian who is aware of the
literary dimension to his *métier* does not presume to be an 'om-
niscient observer' recounting 'the way it really was'; instead he

[3] *Geschichte – Vor den letzten Dingen*, p. 171.
[4] 'Geschichte der Kunst und Historie', p. 192.

prefers to present an occurrence from several different perspectives that may at times contradict rather than complement one another. Moreover, he is wary of fixed beginnings and ends. The origins of opera, for example, cannot be dated as easily as early historians imagined when they allowed the chronological coincidence of the deaths of Palestrina and Lasso and the activities of the Florentine Camerata to mislead them into concluding that it represented an historical chasm, with two epochs openly confronting each other on either side. To avoid the illusion of seamless continuity the modern historian will even upset the course of a narrative by interposing cumbersome and contradictory facts. And he makes us aware that the history he is narrating not only depicts a fragment of the past but documents the present time of writing. For the past is changeable: it is always the past relative to a particular present, and hence is prey to the open-endedness of the future.

Whenever a given fact cannot be adequately explained as a consequence of a particular purpose (i.e. intentionally), or as a case exemplifying a rule (statistically), or as part of an overriding system (functionally), the procedure of historical narration will always seem the most suitable approach, i.e. the fact is made comprehensible by being inserted into a story, whether this story be continuous or discontinuous, in linear or in broken perspective. Admittedly it might be doubted whether a sweeping, comprehensive history – one that depicts events which may well seem rational and purposeful when taken individually but which owe their juxtaposition more to coincidence than to the guidance of that 'end of ends' which Droysen postulated with idealist ardour – can be called narrative at all in the strict sense. Any historian who takes a heaped confusion of actions with no ultimate goal to be a model of historical writing (and it might be difficult to point out the waywardness of this procedure to him) views 'History' as a whole, as opposed to individual histories in particular, as a *mélée* of facts without a subject, facts which are incapable of settling peaceably into a narrative structure. To this sort of historian the past presents itself as a mass of actions, now compatible, now incompatible, that can be understood in individual detail and for short stretches by recourse to intentionality but whose actual consequences were intended by no-one. 'Histories' in the plural, with their individual or collective subjects and their amenability to traditional or modern narrative methods, are subsumed into an all-enveloping 'History' that is a process without subject. It makes eminently good sense to talk about a history of the nineteenth-century tone poem, for example;

and the narrative subject – the tone poem – does have a history in the sense that it underwent changes. Yet these changes that make up its history were in turn offshoots of currents and cross-currents within a larger process which, for its part, had neither goal nor subject. 'Music' writ large does not lend itself as a subject to narrative history.

In a particularly engaging passage of his *Handbuch der Musikgeschichte* Hugo Riemann describes the emergence of the tone poem at the close of the nineteenth century as the upshot of a series of premises that seem neither to be connected with one another nor even to exist on the same plane, whether this plane be subjective intentionality, the history of ideas, or style and technique:

There is no gainsaying that Hector Berlioz gave the post-Beethovenian anti-formalist movements, the striving toward newness *à tout prix*, their initial impetus. For a long while his influence remained slight, being confined to a few isolated composers; and at first the calamitous repercussions that threatened to ensue upon the discrediting of the large forms of the classics were held temporarily in check by the romantic lyricists with their loving absorption in detail and miniature form. It was not until the end of the nineteenth century drew nigh that this *contrebalance* gradually gave way and the onslaught against established ideals began to intensify with noticeable suddenness. This turn of events can only be explained in full if we consider the further developments which took place in opera in the nineteenth century, and in particular the enormous significance of Richard Wagner's music dramas and their steadily mounting influence on the entire musical output of the latter part of the century. Not until his gigantic creations, like Beethoven's symphonic works early in the century, had begun to take paralysing hold of his less talented emulators were new efforts made to strike out on untrodden paths in the field of instrumental music. Now it was that Berlioz came increasingly to the fore. For the French, in the aftermath of the Franco–Prussian War, this probably happened for reasons of patriotic chauvinism, as an attempt to counteract the supremacy which Germany had attained in music on all fronts. In Germany, however, where even today Berlioz's music has made but little headway, it came about for the aforementioned reasons. By the middle years of the nineteenth century classical instrumental music, with its patent epigonism, had already been brought to bankruptcy and forfeited its credit. The symphonic and chamber music of the romantic lyricists gradually paled alongside the attractions of moderate programme music of Liszt's sort and the Slavic and Scandinavian music imported by the Allgemeiner Deutscher Musikverein . . . Finally, and in no small measure, the parties in opposition to the interest recently kindled in early music (initially Bach's) as a result of historical research clamoured for radical innovations in order to force attention onto themselves. The steadily increasing esteem accorded to Brahms, the foremost among those composers who sought renewed contact with the past, was a further goad to this opposition faction to deploy all the means at its disposal in an effort to offset this reversal, and in the event Richard Strauss, on the strength of a series of symphonic poems, was able to gain more ground for the cause of programme music than either Berlioz or Liszt before him (*Handbuch der Musikgeschichte*, II/3: *Die Musik des 18. und 19. Jahrhunderts*, pp. 256–7).

Riemann's text is remarkable for its military images. These demonstrate the unreflecting subservience of music history at that time to political history, which in turn was dictated by the primacy of foreign policy.

In positing a '*contrebalance*' between the lyrical piano piece and the programme symphony, Riemann evidently wishes to say that Berlioz, by sacrificing stability, upset the balance struck between stability and expressiveness in the symphony (a genre so steeped in tradition that the more obvious avenues of innovation were in any case exhausted), but the balance was nevertheless preserved in the lyrical piano piece (a genre almost non-existent in the classical period). Riemann's thesis is questionable, and flawed as an historical construct, on account of its implicit aesthetic judgments. But this only lends all the more credence to his claim that the late-nineteenth-century symphony with its tendency toward programme music was doubly under the influence of Wagner: positively in that it drew on Wagner for its aesthetics and its style; negatively in that composers who chose to write programme music were deliberately avoiding the music drama.

Riemann's argument falls into several layers – from the *ars gallica* to the emergence of Russian and Czech musics (which were set on the path to international recognition precisely by their nationalist traits) and thence to the dialectical conflict between traditionalism and anti-traditionalism. In this respect it bears a stronger resemblance to a report on geological events than to narrative. Indeed, there is some chance of our turning his presentation into a system description, thereby rectifying the impression that a few otherwise unrelated premises have been jumbled together, the end result being the emergence of the symphonic poem. We might, to begin with, assume that the proclamation of an *ars gallica* was linked to the rise of distinctive Russian and Czech musics (there had, of course, been Czech composers in the eighteenth and nineteenth centuries, but no Czech music in the strict sense) by way of mid-nineteenth-century nationalism (there are no grounds for confining nationalism in music to 'peripheral' musical cultures). We

might then go on to assume that the folkloric and nationalist coloration of this music, being a departure into modality from the traditional tonality of art music, gave composers the opportunity to
write music that was popular and, at the same time, progressive in
the manner of Liszt. Finally, we could assume that epigonism in
music lost its aesthetic legitimacy as a result of an aesthetic presup-
position underlying not only the lyrical piano piece but the tone
poem as well – namely the thesis that music's claim to be art resides
in its 'poetic' content, as conceived by Schumann and as formulated
in his critical writings, with this content attaching to a work as an
expression of the unique individuality of its composer. History of
the sort practised by Riemann in the passage quoted above falls
between two stools. It is not narrative history relating to a subject;
Riemann goes beyond this. But neither is it modern structural
history, for however much Riemann may have had this approach in
mind he fell short of its basic principle, merely amassing descriptions of trends instead of linking them.

Now it may seem trivial to claim that 'Music History' writ large is a
process that can be described, at least in part, in terms of the structures of social history or the history of ideas, but cannot be reduced
to a clearly defined subject. In fact, however, this claim is highly
controversial. Jacob Burckhardt's dictum that history takes its
'point of departure' from 'the sufferings, deeds and aspirations of
man as he is, always has been and ever will be'[5] is by no means as
obsolete as rigorous historicists who are obsessed with the notion of
an inexorable, juggernaut march of processes would have us believe. No less a music historian than Jacques Handschin acknowledged his allegiance to Burckhardt's line of thought. From a
methodological standpoint, this emphasis on anthropocentricity
renders it possible to make selections from the chaos of determinable historical facts and to justify those selections: 'History' is
simply whatever impinges significantly upon 'Man', whose nature is
defined by the 'three potencies' – religion, culture and the state.
Objections are not long in forthcoming in an age attuned to
ideological critique. In the first place, the term 'religion' is so various and ramified in its denotations that a sceptic might well find it
less a tangible anthropological constant than a mere empty word.
Furthermore, it seems as though the atrophying of 'religion' is in no
way an absurd prospect but a thoroughly realistic one. Neverthe-

[5] Foreword, *Weltgeschichtliche Betrachtungen.*

less, Burckhardt's dictum has retained a certain empirical relevance within limits which, after all, do happen to encompass several millennia of European history; and an historian in search of a practicable intuitive model need not let radical philosophising undermine this relevance. There is, of course, no contesting the point that when we try to comprehend human evolution in its entirety – a venture still considered feasible in the eighteenth century – the contours of the field begin to blur. Nor can it be denied that in histories of eras spanning decades, or at the most centuries, it is usually the continual changes that impose themselves as a topic on the historian. Yet the most cursory reflection on the premises latent in the day-to-day practice of writing history would suffice to show that Burckhardt's anthropocentric constants have always been implicit in histories of individual periods as an unacknowledged focal point for the historical narrative. A further revelation would be that, however much these constants tend to verge on the unfathomable within universal histories (providing that the history does not stray too far in its methods from the honesty of empiricism), they can still be made the topic of empirical studies within a history of a 'medium' order of magnitude (i.e. one falling somewhere between metaphysical intangibility and heuristic platitude), a history which would bring the unquestionably profound and material changes in a category such as 'art' into proper relation with those enduring elements without which the concept of 'art history' would disintegrate.

In answer to the question whether 'History' has a subject, Karl Marx, in his Paris manuscripts, made the slightly off-colour quip that history as recounted by historians is 'not yet a fully-fledged history of man as a predetermined subject but, at the moment, merely a pro-creative act, being a history solely of his beginnings'.[6] History to date has not been made in a conscious effort toward achieving an overriding end but has arisen by accident as the upshot of actions and series of actions which, taken separately, may seem practical and productive but which in fact have only thwarted each other on the whole. History in the future, on the other hand, will rise above the level of mere 'proto-history' by being the work of men acting in unison toward the realisation of a vision of humanity. In other words, the very philosophy of history that historians find so suspect – with its rapturous speculations on the 'History' of 'Man', or even on 'History' by itself, as though, besides being a

[6] *Frühschriften*, p. 252.

process, it was also the agency behind that process – would seem to anticipate a long hoped for and eminently desirable future state of affairs. 'History' in the singular, which will completely subsume 'histories' in the plural as narrated by historians, is not given us at present; nor is it amenable to the methods of empirical inquiry; but we can and ought to bring it about.

For those who believe in it, the notion of a future history of mankind is already casting its shadow on the methodology of history, even in music history. For in Marxist terms the decisive criterion for the selection of historical facts, i.e. those that 'belong to history' in the strong sense, is their significance for the 'history of man's beginnings', which is to say for the cultivation of his innate capacities, the realisation of which, if it is to be genuine, must be universal in scope. The emphasis falls on art, not for its own sake but for the social function it fulfils – a future function unsullied by the pettinesses of the immediate present, but one which nevertheless must be reconciled with the givens of the present if it is to be realised at all and not simply allowed to degenerate into utopian abstractions.

5

Historicism and tradition

Nietzsche once differentiated between antiquarian, monumental and critical histories. In so doing he created a distinction which, albeit with a different emphasis, forms a central issue in the current controversy over historicism: is historiography a means of assimilating the past or of exercising a critique of tradition? In the popular imagination, the historian is an antiquarian piously absorbed in reconstructing fragments of the past out of an instinctive urge to collect and preserve on the one hand and a desire to escape the pressures of the present on the other. Yet this view is thoroughly onesided. The original motivation behind the development of history as a science lay in the urge, not to master tradition, but to subject it to a rigorous critique. Historicism has its roots in the realisation that a gap exists between the aspirations of the present and the imprint left upon the present by the past.

According to Ferdinand Christian Baur, an eccleciastical historian with Hegelian leanings, it was sixteenth-century Protestantism that produced the form of historical awareness known as 'tradition critique' by counterposing revelation and tradition:

So little credence does a Catholic attach to historical evolution that he views all that has come about over the ages as having existed since the beginnings of time. When Protestants, on the other hand, came to look at their Church, a true sense of history dawned with their realisation that the origins and the later progress of the Church, far from being *a fortiori* identical, were in fact fundamentally different and had to be kept separate (*Die Epochen der kirchlichen Geschichtsschreibung*, p. 40).

A further step toward historical awareness resulted in the late seventeenth and the eighteenth centuries from the *querelle des anciens et des modernes,* the dispute as to whether Antiquity should be given priority over the modern age in literature and art or *vice versa.* In an attempt to settle this conflict of dogmas it was suggested by way of compromise that every age, whether the distant past or the immediate present, must be understood in its own terms rather than measured against another. Admittedly, this compensatory formula bore by and large the appearance of tradition critique, for it nullified, or at any rate impaired, the contention of the classicists that standards for the modern age could be extracted from the legacy of Antiquity. It also meant that the modernists, although unable to have the present recognised as the measure of all ages, were nevertheless successful in advancing their demand to be allowed to draw up their own aesthetic premises rather than remain bound to those of the ancients.

In addition to the religious critique of tradition rooted in Protestantism and its aesthetic counterpart in the *querelle des anciens et des modernes*, there was also a moral critique of tradition that arose during the Enlightenment and drew upon the geographical and anthropological discoveries of the sixteenth to eighteenth centuries. By being exposed to alien cultures, European travellers and travelogue readers were led to look at themselves with greater detachment than hitherto – once, that is, the notion of the 'noble savage' and the existence in China of a sublime ethics free from theology had convinced them of the need to exchange their curiosity-hunter's arrogance for moral involvement. Their own culture lost its aura of uncontested authority. No longer was it the only culture with a claim to rationality and naturalness; instead, it became the object of historical reflection, of tradition critique. The belief that the guiding principles of one's own existence were grounded on an immutable entity known as 'human nature' was shaken by knowledge of other cultures which, though fundamentally alien, could by no means be construed as morally inferior. And now history was scoured for the origins of these principles. The European tradition, whose norms had once seemed unimpeachable for want of comparison with others, lost its exclusive validity. Europeans recognised their own past as being exceptional and particular, having to coexist alongside others of equal stature. No longer was it a single tradition that impinged upon and extended into the present; a variety of traditions now become objects of historical contemplation and, thus objectified, were regarded with detachment. For the historian, whose interests can range with equanimity over Oriental, Chinese or Mexican cultures, the European tradition has no particular priority over other pasts which he might just as easily choose to study. In fact, the investigation of distant cultures can form a methodological model or paradigm by leading ineluctably to that 'controlled estrangement' that Jürgen Habermas demanded from historians in their dealings with the pasts of their own respective cultures.

The trend towards universal history that characterised eighteenth-century historiography, even of the musical sort, was closely tied to a pedagogical premise from historicism, then understood mainly as tradition critique – namely that the process of objectification or detachment from one's own past was a matter less of alienation than of education. Once we recognise the historical nature (i.e. the limitations and alterability) of our basic religious, moral and aesthetic assumptions we rise above the particularity that besets traditionalist, 'pre'-historical thought with its want of self-reflection, and attain that level of awareness that Herder once declared to be – in a qualitative rather than a numerical sense – the level of 'humanity'.

Nietzsche considered the newly won detachment that came from historical awareness as alienation, and derisively remarked that it reduced the historian, with his indiscriminate urge to amass material, to an anthropological 'neuter'. Eighteenth-century humanists, however, greeted this detachment enthusiastically as a process of education. They looked upon preoccupation with the 'otherness' of things foreign and strange from a philosophical rather than a narrowly scientific standpoint, and considered it not an end in itself so much as a passage leading back to the Self – a 'Self', however, which had been made aware of its own particularity through its encounter with history and had thereby put this particularity at least into perspective even if it could not entirely escape it. By recognising the limits of its horizons precisely for what they are – limits – the Self had, paradoxically, crossed them en route to an awareness of 'humanity'. Admittedly objectifying tradition necessarily implies detachment, 'tradition' being taken as that part of the past that impinges on the present. In the eighteenth century, however, detachment was not viewed as alienation, as a way of losing oneself in the other, so much as a first step that was to be followed by a second one in the opposite direction, in which that portion of tradition that had given rise to this process in the first place would be assimilated anew and thereby 'de-alienated'. Moreover, the detachment stage being now complete along with its attendant self-estrangement, this act of reassimilation would, it was thought, elevate particularity into universality. Or such at least was the intention.

This idea of a type of education resulting from a dialectical process of detachment and assimilation was discarded, or relegated to the backbenches of popular history, by nineteenth-century historicism. Tradition critique and the notion of a universal history went with it. As Hans Freyer put it, world history collapsed into a world history of Europe. History – meaning recollection of one's own past as institutionalised into a science – was expected to involve not so much detachment from the assumptions underlying one's own existence as confirmation of one's own nature. States of affairs in real life could, it was hoped, be understood by reconstructing their origins. Of course other cultures were studied as before, but as part of a new field separate and distinct from history: ethnology. Nor was preoccupation with the strange and alien carried on with the same passionate commitment as in the eighteenth century; interest in such things betrayed less a sense of anthropological involvement than a neutral, positivist stance. Unimaginably remote subjects were studied with no consequent effect on self-awareness. The idea of inculcating a sense of humanity through 'alienation' was dead. In the nineteenth century, universals were sought, if at all, by enlarging upon nationalist traits such as musicians thought to find in Weber and Chopin no less than in Smetana and Mussorgsky.

A few tattered remains of the bond that once existed between tradition critique, universal history and the idea of humanity can be found in a half-suppressed music-theoretical controversy over the tonal systems of alien cultures that Fétis, Helmholtz and Ellis touched upon without actually pursuing to a conclusion. It is a notion firmly ingrained in music theory and in music history alike that the tonal harmony characteristic of post-medieval European music has its roots in the immutable nature of music and the human constitution. This notion would doubtless have been discarded in the nineteenth century if the historical thought of that time had still been under the threefold influence of tradition critique, universal history and the concept of education as detachment: the first showing that all seemingly natural and rational things have their historical basis and will alter with time; the second that foreign cultures also have their claim to a philosophy of history; and the third that by distancing ourselves from our own previous history we transcend particularity and reach the level of humanity. With the demise of the Enlightenment, however, any strange or puzzling phenomena that rubbed against the grain of the prevailing system were merely noted down; no obligation was felt to draw consequences from them. Being entirely European in scope, the music theory drawn upon by historians of the time remained unchallenged.

Yet, in all fairness to nineteenth-century history, we must distinguish between a 'substantive' tradition critique bent on rooting out prejudices, and a 'methodological' one in which distrust of surviving historical narratives was, so to speak, institutionalised. Nineteenth-century historicists practised this latter form of tradition critique to excess. No matter how pious their attempt to reconstruct rather than criticise the past ('past' meaning largely one's own previous history), earlier observers and commentators were treated with remorseless suspicion. Tradition, meaning that part of the past that extends into and endures within the present, was supposed to be preserved in spirit by subjecting the letter of its sources to a critique of such severity that the philological and historical process often took on the character of a cross-examination.

The twentieth century has seen a persistent decline in the confidence shown in historical reflection as a means of ascertaining the assumptions and principle categories behind our moral and aesthetic existence. Nor is there any apparent hope of reviving the eighteenth-century ideal of education, the belief that particularity is elevated to humanity by self-detachment. At the same time a conviction is spreading that histories that touch upon all available topics with perfect equanimity are in fact, as Nietzsche had suspected, a sign of alienation. It might however be remarked in passing that the aesthetic pleasure afforded by sweeping overviews of the past – the 'wide-angle' view of history, to put it pejoratively – need not be scorned and reviled (as it so often is in current polemical attacks on the nineteenth-century concept of education) as a motive for studying history, however insufficient it may be to warrant history's existence as an institution. Nor is the desire to avoid the pressures of the present – a desire which political zealots consider tantamount to immorality – to be despised as a means of stimulating interest in history, though of course it remains one's own private affair and can never be the *raison d'être* of a discipline with pretences to being a public institution.

In recent years it has become a matter of common opinion that history, by objectifying the past, leads to alienation from the past and thus undermines the very tradition it was meant to draw upon. This opinion at once reflects a reaction against the historical method and expresses the fear that we are still in its clutches. Tradition critique is advanced as a motive for studying history, but without the enthusiasm that accompanied it in the eighteenth century; and there is much secret mourning for the nineteenth century when history, still in the full bloom of health, was taken to be a process of reassimilating the substance of tradition by criticising surviving historical records. History, to put it bluntly, seems to the more philosophically adept of its detractors to be a deficient sub-species of tradition, just as in Heidegger's *Sein und Zeit* the 'ready-at-hand', i.e. things perceived and recognised as objects, is a deficient sub-species of the 'ready-to-hand', the things we encounter in daily life.

So it seems that history and tradition are drifting asunder, with historical awareness remaining backward wherever tradition persists and, conversely, tradition crumbling wherever historical awareness takes hold. However, there will be no solving this problem if we simply dismiss it as 'bourgeois' and use empty Marxist catchphrases to invoke a dialectical unity of historical consciousness and 'substantive tradition'.[1] Instead, so as not to fall behind in this dispute, we should take as our starting point the historicism question in the context put forward by Hans-Georg Gadamer in *Wahrheit und Methode*. Tradition, according to Gadamer, is less a well-defined aggregate of things surviving into the present with an objective, concrete meaning to be divined than a 'process of transmission' in which the contemplator of history 'participates'. In these terms, the historian who wishes to understand history 'from within' must project himself into the tradition he is studying, not however, by abstracting or disowning his own basic assumptions

[1] Weimann, *Literaturgeschichte und Mythologie*, p. 51.

but simply by being who he is (anyone who tries to 'project himself' into another's position cannot escape the fact that it is 'himself' that he is projecting). By objectifying tradition, and thereby making it the object of history, we do not detach ourselves from tradition, whether this be the tradition we have grown up in or a foreign tradition we wish to adopt. Rather, we gain one means of ascertaining just what it is about this tradition that gives it its distinctive character. The historian does not treat tradition as a distant object; he feels enveloped by it, caught in its sway. And to ignore the normative claims of tradition, as Wilhelm Dilthey demanded, for the sake of objectivity, is, Gadamer maintains, out of place in history. To begin with, religion, philosophy and aesthetics are also part of history, and cannot be extracted from it without doing violence to its meaning. But furthermore, even the most disinterested of historians can never completely eradicate the prejudices that, while hindering him, nevertheless make him who he is; indeed it would be foolish for him to try (a central portion of Gadamer's book is devoted to a vindication of prejudice, intended to demonstrate its legitimacy). To Gadamer's way of thinking, *Verstehen* in history means achieving a *rapprochement* between the demands of tradition and the historian's own assumptions: a text is not 'understood' until one reaches an 'understanding' with it about its material content. On the whole, Gadamer's presentation seems to be an attempt to restore the close ties that once existed between the historical method and tradition, from which it had become estranged.

Still, the difficulties that await the historian who adopts the premises and conclusions of Gadamer's line of thought should on no account be taken lightly. To begin with, it not infrequently happens (despite Gadamer's assumption to the contrary) that historians find the thought and behaviour of remote epochs the more incomprehensible and mystifying the more deeply they probe into the past. Secondly, Gadamer seems less to be describing the realities of historical research than to be outlining its possibilities. Agreed, it is an exaggeration bordering on absurdity to suspect each and every instance of 'objectification' (*Vergegenständlichung*), in which our unreflected dealings with something give way to detached observation, of amounting to 'alienation' (*Entfremdung*). But there is no denying that when history is reduced to mere research technique it quite often oversteps the bounds at which that form of objectification that still leaves open the possibility of reassimilation turns into what the Marxists call 'reification' (*Verdinglichung*), which is at root little better than indifference masquerading as industry.

Thirdly, it is not clear to what extent dialogue structure – whose characteristics Gadamer presupposes for his argument – provides an adequate model of the way to gain historical knowledge. However inappropriate it may be in a conversation to analyse our interlocutor's mind instead of reaching agreement as to the material validity or invalidity of what he is saying, we are nevertheless perfectly justified in reconstructing the assumptions and motives implicit in works of history. What would he want of urbanity in a conversationalist is entirely warranted in an historian, who is at full liberty to play the detective. In daily affairs, ignoring what someone is saying and instead diverting his attention by asking why he is saying it can at best be condoned as a roundabout means to the end of reaching agreement on the points in question; in history however it can be an end in itself.

Fourthly, Gadamer apparently fails to note that historical detachment does not always nullify or renounce the claim of a work of art to exist for its own sake as an aesthetic presence rather than merely to be analysed as a document on some past state of affairs. Indeed, an awareness of the historical remoteness of a piece of music can become part of the act of perception without thereby belittling or obstructing the aesthetic qualities of the work.

Lastly, Gadamer's claim that historical thought can never be entirely free of assumptions but will always be grounded in tradition, which in turns serves as the object of inquiry, fails to take into account the distinctions between tradition critique and reassimilation. Even of we grant that tradition, or at any rate the historian's own tradition, is at once the object and the premise of history, we still beg the question as to whether by objectifying tradition we come closer to it or retreat from it. Gadamer's contention that historical thought is itself historical in its influence and impact carries no weight in an apology for the priority of the element of reassimilation, for the very act of reflecting on historical influence can diminish that influence by holding it up to scrutiny and criticism.

Historical thought rests on a dichotomy. On the one hand, as memory institutionalised into a science, it represents a form of tradition; on the other, by using a form of objectification that amounts to 'controlled estrangement', it stands in opposition to unbroken traditionalism. To this contradiction between history as assimilation of the past and as tradition critique we must add a further distinction in the case of music history, where historicism as an academic pursuit cannot be understood and analysed independently of historicism in musical practice.

For 'musical historicism' – the term is not, nor need be, used pejoratively – is a mode both of thought and of behaviour. As a mode of thought it is characterised by the conviction that a musical creation is, as Adorno put it, 'historical through and through' – in other words that historicity is not simply a fundamental basis for all musical creations but actually forms their inmost essence. To an historian who is not fearful of taking conclusions to their extremes – and extremes that once seemed paradoxical have become wellnigh trivial in recent decades – the concept of classicism (in the aesthetic rather than the historical sense) and the concept of naturalness are both equally suspect, and the notion that significant works of music stand apart from history, preserving their aesthetic content independently of the historical context in which they originated, is metaphysically naive. Furthermore, the givens of the material world that were, in earlier times, thought to provide music with its foundations, collapsed in the age of historicism into a few scattered remains, where they were not simply denied wholesale. At the beginning of our century, for instance, the essence of music was held to reside in tonal harmony, which accordingly could be tampered with only at the price of turning musical sense into nonsense. Later this function passed to the opposition of consonance and dissonance. Finally, nothing was left but the ordering of intervals according to their degree of 'sonance' – an ordering void of specific distinctions because it proved in the end to be a matter of historical convention, of compositional technique, rather than the underlying material of music.

If historicism as a mode of thought is characterised in a negative sense by its disavowal of natural norms and a belief that aesthetic content stands outside history, historicism in musical practice refers to nothing more than the predominance of the old over the new. This predominance is regarded as a burden: the word 'museum', heard in aesthetic discussions, expresses weariness or even hatred of things cultural. The overwhelming preponderance of earlier works in our concert halls and opera houses has the disastrous consequence for the avant-garde of hindering proper performances of new music, both in number and in quality. This imbalance is regarded as restrictive and inhibiting, and 'historicism', when applied to musical practice, takes on pejorative connotations foreign to the academic sense of the word. It serves a defensive function, being intended to denounce its own object.

Historicism as a mode of thought and historicism in practice need not coincide. We can immerse ourselves in the past and reach a sympathetic understanding of it without necessarily wishing to re-create it – though obviously music historians will feel an urge to communicate their discoveries to the world of music lovers. Or, conversely, we can try to reconstruct part of the past on the concert platform without being convinced that music is 'historical through and through'. Thought and practice might even be so much at variance as to put the expression 'historicism' in a shady light.

Anyone who seeks to vindicate the preponderance of old music over new in our concert and opera repertories will generally turn to anything but historicism as a mode of thought to support his claims. For, granted that music is 'historical through and through', it follows that the expressive content of even the greatest musical masterpieces is mutable and transitory, and hence of little value in an apology for the predominance of early music – or at any rate of less value than the opposing 'unhistorical' belief in the timelessness and 'classicism' of great music. Aesthetic Platonism – i.e. a tendency to place works of music in a sort of extratemporal, superlunary realm – has become the popular aesthetic of a public that feels at home with earlier music but distrusts or even abominates the new. This Plato-nism is the mainstay of the convervatism of present-day concert- and opera-goers who, sensing in academic history a tendency towards tradition critique, incline to regard it with suspicion.

In the eyes of the traditionalists, the idea of the extratemporal and classical is closely allied to that of naturalness in music. In the nine-teenth century, musical classicism was a nationalist phenomenon born of the fusion of the 'early classics', Bach and Handel, with the Viennese classics, a fusion which in turn was viewed as an artificial consummation of a natural musical process whose origins could be traced to folksong. Both classicism and the adherence to folk music – i.e. the belief that 'nature' and the 'classical' are equally timeless – fall under the rubric of the 'national spirit' hypothesis. In our cent-ury, by contrast, appeals to naturalness in music largely serve polemical ends. The alleged real nature of music is always given special emphasis whenever new music, whether atonal, serial or electronic, is meant to be cordoned off and stigmatised. In music theory, conservatism reveals itself with particular clarity to be what it has been since the days of Edmund Burke – a counter-ideology.

If historicism in practice tends accordingly toward a popular Platonist aesthetic in which the classical and natural stand above and apart from history, historicism as a mode of thought has given rise to

a distrust of restoration or naive traditionalism. In historical hermeneutics as conceived by Schleiermacher and Dilthey the distance
that separates us from the past appears greater, not less, as our
knowledge of the past increases. Understanding that is alleged to
be direct almost invariably proves to be false; and the indirect
method of *Verstehen* that draws on hermeneutics as a basis for
understanding art reveals a past that appears strange and dis-
concerting rather than familiar and approachable.

However, an historian who views early music as the expression of
an age far removed from ours in spirit, if not altogether extinct, will
view with suspicion the naivety of any attempt to reconstruct the
past in musical practice without qualifications and caveats. Instinctively as he may wish to translate his historical insights into audible
sounds, he knows that misrepresentation is unavoidable. He is too
clearly aware of the disturbing dialectics at work – the fact that
increased understanding in history goes hand in hand with an ever
greater sense of difference and alienness – ever to trust the un-
abashed practitioner of music in the arsenal of history. There is no
escape in sight from the dilemma that to feel close to things past is
to misconstrue them, while to understand them is to sense their
remoteness.

Yet by distancing himself from the past the historian clears a
path for the new. It is possible without distortion to draw from the
historicist thesis of the substantive historicality of works of music
the conclusion that an age should look to its own music for its
reflection instead of clinging doggedly to music of the past. (The
fact that today's public treats the music of the eighteenth and nineteenth centuries as its own is so taken for granted that we scarcely
notice just how strange and paradoxical this situation actually is.)
Historicism as a mode of thought is certainly not irreconcilable with
the spirit of the avant-garde; indeed, the two complement rather
than contradict one another. Anyone who openly espouses the
view that music is 'historical through and through' will have to
regard present-day significance as the fundamental basis of the artistic experience. Nor is it a contradiction in terms for an historian
to confront new music with the same impartiality and reverence
that he accords music of the past: historical reflection, insofar as its
emphasis falls on tradition critique, implicitly contains a *parti pris*
for the avant-garde.

Returning to Gadamer's premises outlined above, it might be
objected that to 'historicise' artistic perception entirely would be to
violate its true purpose and meaning. Anyone who claims to grasp

the essence of a piece of music (so the argument runs) by experiencing its contemporary relevance, i.e. its appropriateness to a particular moment in time or what Adorno called its historiological 'attunement', misses the point and mistakes the mere deciphering of a musical creation as a document on the *Zeitgeist* or historical 'level of consciousness' for a true appreciation of it as art. For even if this deciphering were to provide a complete 'explanation' of a piece it would still not come to grips with it as art: the exchange of categories, from work to document, would be an infringement of the rights of music as an art form, which are the rights that warrant its existence.

This argument, however, has its flaws. In the case of new music, for instance, it might well turn out that the 'historicising' type of aesthetic experience is not, in fact, imposed from without but is fully in keeping with the nature and objectives of this music, i.e. that we should listen to new music with an ear to contemporary relevance rather than classicity, to the insights that a new work affords into its time of origin rather than its chances of outliving that time. Accordingly, this mode of experience, far from betokening the decline of aesthetic perception, may in fact represent a thoroughly legitimate approach of its own, however limited in historical scope. (In other words, it is not only the content of aesthetic perception which alters with time but also its categorical structure, i.e. that which makes it possible at all.) On the other hand, this means that transposing the 'historicisation' trend mindlessly from modern music theory – where, not coincidentally, it arose – to earlier periods is just as wrongheaded as Gadamer's assumptions would suggest; and conversely that Gadamer's own argument is guilty of ignoring or distorting a significant part of twentieth-century music by maintaining a concept of classical timelessness. Theories of historicism, whether Gadamer's with its stress on assimilation of tradition, or its opposite in which the emphasis falls on tradition critique, evidently need to be historicised themselves before they can become plausible.

Scarcely less ambiguous than the ideas surrounding the concepts of 'historicism' and 'historical thought' is their counterpart, 'tradition', which can refer either to the legacy of the past that has survived unquestioned into the present or to a conscious assimilation of this legacy. (It would be a doctrinaire exaggeration to magnify the slight distinction between tradition and conservatism, meaning a conscious effort to retain and preserve, into a gaping chasm by stressing solely the lack of consciousness inherent in pre-conservative traditionalism.) Accordingly, critique of tradition by means of historical objectification and 'controlled estrangement' varies in its emphasis as the notion of tradition changes character: either it reveals standards once considered natural in equal proportion to their conventionality to be by-products of history that we can alter or discard at will; or, by engendering a sense of detachment from tradition, it creates problems for the once seemingly straightforward process of assimilation by raising doubts as to whether this process does justice to the material content of the past on the one hand or to the current situation on the other.

Once we no longer simply allow tradition to 'happen' beyond our notice but make it the object of reflection – and this not merely in terms of its content, as the sum total of things inherited from the past, but also in a formal sense, as a process with a definite structure – tradition takes on the appearance of history of reception. This achieved, it is equally or even more interesting to discover how things are passed down as tradition, rather than what these things are; and changes or adaptations in these things that once passed unnoticed now become objects of special attention. However, once unreflected tradition has been transformed into a 'reflected', or rather progressively 'more reflected' tradition, it becomes difficult to view change with customary traditionalist equanimity. Instead, we feel forced to choose between propagating change with progressive ardour, or hindering it in a conservative spirit, or even reversing it out of fondness for the old order. Naive traditionalism metamorphoses into other forms of behaviour toward the legacy of the past.

One sure sign of unbroken tradition is a devotion to 'established truths'. Here the question never arises as to whether the age of a thing establishes its validity or, conversely, whether a particular norm has existed from time immemorial simply because it happens to be true. Convention and validity are so inextricably fused together as to obviate the need to reflect on how they came about at all or which, logically or chronologically, preceded the other. By comparison, the belief that norms are grounded in the nature of things constitutes a step towards rationality by enlarging upon the earlier form of traditionalism, which made no distinction between the natural and the conventional but identified the one with the other. The Enlightenment suspected traditions of being arbitrary and at odds with nature and rationality, and thus sundered what naive traditionalists thought to be inseparably linked. Only in reaction to this development did traditionalists feel compelled to

advance distinctions of their own, invoking by way of self-justifi-
cation either the nature of the physical world and its immutability
(as in the case of tonal harmony) or the venerable age that grants
convention its validity (as when the Palestrina style was made the
standard of authentic church music).

In the eighteenth century historicists plumbed the origins of
traditions in order to prove them transitory and fallible, and
erected 'natural systems' in opposition to mere arbitrary conventions. Both endeavours involved a certain amount of tradition critique. In naive traditionalism, however, convention and validity
merged into an undifferentiated whole. Once these formerly
inseparable factors had been irretrievably sundered traditionalists
were forced, if they wished to argue their position at all, to base
their legitimacy on standards whose naturalness was vouchsafed by
great antiquity or on conventions validated by the depth of their
historical roots. The polemical argument against traditions, for its
part, could either elevate naturalness and rationality to norms in
order to expose tradition as convention, and convention in turn as
arbitrary; or it could take up an historicist line of reasoning and
point out that the age of a rule or custom is not an indication of
unimpeachable validity so much as a sign of increasing remoteness
from and foreignness to the spirit of the present.

Now, a sense of tradition, an undying and unquestioning faith in
the authority of our legacy from the past, is not exclusively a way of
looking at the past. Its concern is also – perhaps even primarily –
the present and the future. Those who feel guided and sheltered by
standards, institutions and habitual patterns of perception from
previous centuries will likewise feel a sense of confidence in the
present and, at the same time, foresee a future that differs little
from the present. It would scarcely have been possible for historical
thought to supplant and supersede traditionalism as a mode of perceiving the past if this further function served by traditionalism,
namely to substantiate a consciousness of the present and the
future, had not been usurped by an idea that stands in direct conflict with faith in authority: the idea of progress. This enthusiasm
for the future, which degenerated in our century into what Ernst
Bloch has called the 'hope principle', seems to be a substitute for
the trust once felt in the permanence and resilience of tradition,
even serving an analogous function of establishing a consciousness
of the present. To put it another way, in the nineteenth century the
functions once fulfilled by traditionalism in conveying a sense of
the present and the future were, in a manner of speaking, parcelled

out between historicism and the idea of progress, the one soberly detached from the past, the other enthusiastically compensating for the metaphysical deficiency that resulted as the past was stripped of its mythical aura under the rigours of historical thought.

Hence naive traditionalism – mute submission to the authority of all that used to be, which was cherished less for being 'past' than for being merely 'longstanding' – gave way in the nineteenth century to other patterns of behaviour towards tradition such as conservatism or the impulse to restore.

Lest we invite distortion, we must not treat tradition and restoration as identical. They differ first in that the former has an immediate relation to the past, the latter an intermediate and secondary one. Tradition presupposes seamless continuity, and is often likened to an unbroken chain in this respect; restoration, on the other hand, is an attempt to renew contact with a tradition that has been interrupted or has atrophied. In the nineteenth century, the works of Mozart and Beethoven were part of a living tradition, whereas the music of Palestrina and Bach, despite a few slender threads of tradition, was the object of restoration. And it is this element of restoration, not merely distance in time, that determines whether or not a work is to be considered 'early music': the inner, rather than the outward, merely chronological distance, is the deciding factor. In 1829, a century after its time of writing, Bach's St Matthew Passion already belonged to 'early music'; Beethoven's symphonies, after a century and a half, have yet to acquire this status.

Secondly, restorations, unlike traditions, are by their very nature reflective. It was no accident that nineteenth-century efforts to reinstate 'truth' and 'purity' in church music by falling back on the Palestrina style – which even Prostestants lauded as exemplary – and on Gregorian chant in its original form were accompanied by a vast profusion of apologetic literature and polemical diatribe against church music in its fallen state. Restorations are plagued by the contradiction that the 'original' and 'unspoilt' can only be reconstituted by generously stretching the meanings of these terms. They are, as Schiller put it, 'sentimental', whereas unbroken traditions are 'naive'. So long as a tradition is still in full flower it is taken for granted and needs no further justification. Beethoven, for instance, was fully convinced that the thorough-bass ought to be accepted without a murmur as the quintessential basic rule of all composition. Tradition is its own vindication. No-one in the seven-

teenth or eighteenth centuries expected the rule prohibiting parallel fifths to be supported by rational argument; the belief,
ingrained by tradition, that they sound 'bad' had become second
nature in listening to music, a self-evident and incontestable fact.
But the more deeply tradition is rooted in the unconscious, the
more disrupting become all attempts at change, which listeners, in
their initial anger, regard as a sign not of evolution but of wanton
destruction. The clearest indication that a tradition has been
broken is the outraged response that a certain acoustical creation
masquerading as music is in fact not music at all but 'diabolical
clamour', 'cynical mockery', or mere noise. The dissolution of
tonality at the hands of Schoenberg, the breakdown of metrical
rhythm at the hands of Stravinsky, the collapse of musical form to
momentary sound in Webern or the suppression of pitch by noise in
electronic music – all these owed their shock value to the destruction of norms of whose existence outraged listeners had till then
scarcely been conscious. Self-evident truths taken utterly for
granted were challenged unawares.

Thirdly, all restorations, even the seemingly successful ones, run
the risk that the musical idiom to be reconstituted will forfeit its
substance and expressiveness in its new surroundings – a risk used
to good advantage by Stravinsky. Furthermore, in its 'second life',
any element from the past, particularly if its restoration affects the
current practice of composition, almost invariably has an aura of
the 'sentimental', and this time not in Schiller's sense of the word
but in the pejorative everyday sense. The reconstructed nineteenth-century Palestrina style of Eduard Grell and Michael
Haller, when it did not simply devolve into technical exercises,
inadvertently took on the appearance of a musical reminiscence of
the long-lost past; for all their deliberate efforts toward rigour and
objectivity, a vein of nostalgia is unmistakable. Indeed, this aesthetic impression can be traced to tangible features in technique.
The sixteenth-century ecclesiastical modes changed character
when they were transplanted to the nineteenth century. To a
listener steeped in the tradition of tonal harmony they appear as
deviations from, or as expressive or picturesque variants of, the
standard major and minor modes. Being a variant of the minor
sixth degree, the 'Dorian' sixth has an expressive dimension that
did not attach to the old church mode until the nineteenth century.
And the fact that the church modes were considered as deviations
rather than self-sufficient is the technical correlate to the 'sentimental' trait that lent the reconstituted Palestrina style its

romantic tinge. This increase of expressiveness in the Palestrina style is offset by a corresponding loss of expressiveness noted, and exploited, by Stravinsky in the case of Pergolesi, or Pseudo-Pergolesi. The common element behind these two seemingly contradictory processes is the reversal of the original essence of their respective musical idioms.

In addition to traditionalism, in which the past extends unnoticed into the present, and the trend towards restoration of things already extinct, there also exists a musical brand of conservatism which, like its political counterpart, did not develop into the form understood by the present-day term until the nineteenth century. Conservative thought and behaviour, unlike attempts at restoration, aim not so much at reviving defunct traditions as at preserving still living ones. However, the traditions are no longer maintained with the same unquestioning faith as in traditionalist periods; instead, conservative thought is reflective, and even contains a hidden polemical trait, as the traditions to be upheld are felt to be endangered and the manner of vindicating them by rational argument has been borrowed from the enemy camp of progressive liberalism. Conservatism manifests itself as traditionalism under the new conditions of an anti-traditionalist age. The tenacity with which Brahms clung to sonata form, not as a formula but as a principle or ideal, despite the fact that since 1830 it had seemed obsolete and devoid of meaning, is the mark of a conservative but by no means epigonal nature. His reflective turn of mind, his stubborn, almost perverse insistence on preserving a part of tradition in the face of the dominant spirit of the times, the despised 'New German' school – who could overlook this side to Brahms's character? In his technique he fought against the decay of form seemingly manifest in Liszt's symphonic poems; in his aesthetic he stood opposed to the then pervading trend towards programme music. This is not to say that he left the sonata form as he had found it; but the modifications in the means he employed served the larger end of preserving, under altered conditions, the meaning of this form as a structure as large in scale as it was perfect in consistency and coherence.

(By 1850 or thereabouts key structure had become so refined, and so weakened by colouristic uses of harmony, as to lose the fundamental significance that it had had for Haydn and Beethoven. Its role as an element of cohesion was taken over by thematic and motivic development, now spread over entire movements instead of being concentrated in development sections. Covering sonata movements with a fine mesh of motivic relations, or with half-latent diastematic associations, compensated for the absence of clear form-giving properties in the key system and at the same time represented a 'logical' counterpart to the poeticising and programmatic inclinations of the age.)

In aesthetic perception, conservative efforts to maintain tradition by altering the letter so as to preserve the spirit take the form of a tendency to see in the changing interpretations of musical works nothing more than contingent manifestations of an eternally unvarying substance, adapted to particular moments in history. Authentic conservatism is by no means as inflexible as its detractors claim; but it does reject the notion that music is 'historical through and through', insisting instead on distinguishing between central properties that are supposedly inviolable, and peripheral ones that are interchangeable.

Conservatism turns into historicism the moment the survival into the present of things past is subjected to scrutiny, and this scrutiny leads to a conviction or feeling that past things form an essential part of the present precisely in being from the past, and not because of some substance within them that has withstood all change. The historical faculty that analyses works of music in the context of their time of origin should be taken virtually intact into the aesthetic experience; the two should not be kept apart by a rigid compartmentalisation of art into its aesthetic and documentary aspects. Awareness of the past is not incompatible with aesthetic presence; on the contrary, it can be a component part of that presence. The historicist firmly believes that what a work has to say about the age in which it was written belongs at one and the same time to the past and the present, not because works are 'timeless' but because past and present form an indissoluble alloy. The past is what has survived from the past, and hence is part and parcel of the present. The works that have extended from earlier periods into our own age do not come solitary and sequestered; they bring their own time – a *temps perdu* – along with them. The naive traditionalist clings to a metaphysics of timeless beauty in the abstract, the conservative to the belief that behind the various manifestations of a thing there lies an unchanging and inviolable substance; but the historicist, with his Schillerean 'sentimental' leanings, enjoys past things for being past, in a form of recollection that figures as an essential feature of the present moment. The remote is perceived as such but experienced as near; the foreign is recognised as alien yet felt to be familiar. The ultimate message of historicism is a twisted aesthetic paradox.

Aestheticising the historical and historicising the aesthetic are opposite sides of the same coin. As meaning in art is felt more and more to
bear the stamp of history, and in extreme cases to be 'historical
through and through', there arises a corresponding tendency to view
history not so much as the preliminary build-up to the present and
one's own existence but rather as a broad panorama to be gazed upon
in aesthetic contemplation. The distinction between the aesthetic
and the documentary sides of art is no longer as sharp and uncompromising as aesthetic theory had made it out to be. With sufficient
detachment we can even note a close connection between the
emancipation of art towards aesthetic autonomy and the tendency to
read works of art as documents, and can recognise them as being part
of one and the same historical process: the decline of the immediate
practical functions that had existed in sacred and court art. Not only
did historical and aesthetic thought originate at the same time, in the
eighteenth century; they also belong, the documentary versus aesthetic distinction notwithstanding, to the same current in the history
of ideas. Both are new ways of approaching works of art in a spirit of
objectivity and detachment following the downfall of those practical functions that Heinrich Besseler had in mind when, drawing
upon Heidegger's concept of the 'ready-to-hand', he referred to
'everyday music' (*Umgangsmusik*). This downfall was manifested
not in an open suppression of functional *Gebrauchsmusik*, which in
fact is even today undergoing mass production, but in a prevailing
belief that the function of a work bears a distorted if not contrary
relation to its artistic character and aesthetic value – a belief deliberately disseminated by the prevailers and adopted by those who were
prevailed upon.

6

Hermeneutics in history

Verstehen, the principal methodological category of history in the
nineteenth and early twentieth centuries, seems latterly to have
fallen into disrepute. Modern historians with their predilection for
social history no longer try primarily to account for the intentions,

motives and ideas of historical agents, preferring instead to determine the trends and forces to which these agents were subject. Still, insufficient as the interpretation of intentions has proved to be as a basis for writing history, it is no less indisputable that we must understand the sense of an action before undertaking a causal or functional analysis of the conditions under which it came about and exercised its influence.

The *Verstehen* theory of history as developed in the nineteenth century was based, implicitly or explicitly, on the notion of an imaginary dialogue that the historian conducted with historical agents in an effort to discover their aims and motives. To keep this dialogue from degenerating into a cross-examination, an exchange of monologues, or mere palaver, certain conditions had to be observed which, despite or precisely because of their triviality, were not infrequently neglected and hence warrant discussion here. A dialogue, then, presupposes a common language, agreement on a matter in question, and an effort to understand the interlocutor as something more than a mere object of scrutiny: as an individual with a distinct personality.

These component features of dialogue are mutually dependent on one another. Just how closely agreement on language is bound up with agreement on a matter in question is shown, negatively, by the difficulties we encounter when we try to explain technical terms without at the same time showing how to handle the objects they are meant to stand for. By the same token, any aspect of reality that we wish to grasp has been formed in advance by language, which supplies the categories in which we perceive and interpret that reality. Tiresome as it might be to explain pitch to an alien listener who perceived and defined differences of frequency as degrees of brightness or loudness, it is no less difficult for us to abandon the metaphorical system that we have grown up with and perceive auditory phenomena according to any category but our deep-seated one of pitch.

A sometimes tortuous dialectic exists between reaching agreement on a matter in question and trying to understand our interlocutor. True, it would be thoroughly wrongheaded and even callous to bypass the matter in question entirely and analyse solely the personality of our interlocutor on the devious basis of the points he is trying to make, i.e. to ignore the plausibility or implausibility of his accounts and arguments and to concentrate exclusively on what hints he lets slip about his character. Yet sometimes we cannot avoid putting ourselves in another's position and reconstructing his

motives for speaking in order to understand his points. This altern-
ating emphasis on the individual and the matter in question forms a
sort of hermeneutic circle: from a person's comments we draw conclusions about his personality, only to use them in turn to understand his comments more fully and assess their validity more precisely. There is a mutual and reciprocal relation between ends and
means in agreeing on the matter and understanding the individual;
the important thing is to maintain the balance between them rather
than letting one get the upper hand.

In an age of suspicion, as ours most certainly is, it is not easy to
argue the point that we stand a greater chance of learning something by sympathising and involving ourselves with our interlocutor
than by mistrusting him. Letting ill-temper be the basic posture of
historical inquiry is, of course, characteristic of that style of positivism which is modelled on the cross-examination of witnesses;
but it is equally characteristic of an ideological critique which
knows no rest until it has reduced lofty ideals into shoddy, if unconscious, interests. The spirit of our times seems to have found its
most apt expression in those tribunals in which guilt is assumed
until innocence is proved.

An ability to sympathise with others rather than remain fixated
with oneself and one's own problems, though of less use to a philosopher, is part of the historian's basic intellectual equipment. This
would scarcely need mentioning were it not that the historian's
need to project himself into the position of the historical agents of
some earlier age, while considered a commonplace a few decades
ago, has in the meantime been fundamentally called into question
and suspected of being ideologically motivated. Modern historians
no longer believe in the 'general ego' of humanity that Droysen
spoke of, but rather in unbridgeable gulfs separating ages and
ethnic and social groups. No doubt it is questionable and naive to
see in every historical agent the 'man pure and simple' as a potential
subject for the novelist's art; but it would be crippling to have an
historical conscience so sceptical and hypersensitive as to remain
unassuaged until the last glimmer of common human sentiment
had been removed and the past made to appear inaccessibly distant
and alien.

The somewhat threadbare but in no way resolved controversy
over *Verstehen* as opposed to *Erklären* – i.e. understanding versus
explaining, or inward versus outward interpretation – can be qualified somewhat in a discipline centring primarily on artificial music
by pointing out the far-reaching historical changes undergone in

the object to be understood or explained. The contested notion
that an historian must project himself into the minds of historical
agents if he wishes to grasp history from 'within' rather than merely
chronicle its external manifestations presupposes, in the case of
music, that in the last analysis it is the composer's intentions, resulting from his private feelings and sentiments, that determine
what form music will take and what meaning it will have. This
assumption is, however, not as unassailable and self-evident as it
might appear to historians who have grown up with the aesthetic
principles of the 'great age of art' – in the case of music, the period
from the late eighteenth century to the early twentieth. Indeed, the
object to be understood or explained – the auditory creation that
we confront or perceive within frames of reference that are integral
to the study of music – has been variously characterised and its
features variously emphasised even within post-medieval artificial
music, let alone in the musics of remote ages, societies or peoples.
Consequently the idea springs naturally to mind of adapting our
historical method to suit the various transformations of the
phenomena under study.

With due allowance for simplification we can make a rough distinction between a functional, a representational, a personal and a
structural view as to what constitutes the primary substance of music,
and hence the main subject matter of music history. These distinctions imply only that the emphasis shifted with each new age of
music history, not that older views were suppressed wholesale by
their successors. In the artificial music of the nineteenth century,
when the originality ideal was in full sway, the element of function
was by no means irrelevant, however much it had been forced to
sidelines (music with a function ran the risk of degenerating into
trivial music). Similarly, the representational view of the meaning
or content of music did not disappear in the age of expression,
though it did lose the aesthetic prestige that it had enjoyed in the
mid eighteenth century when the 'pictorial genre', which included
not only tone painting but baroque allegory and figure as well,
became obsolete.
    The notion of function dominated sixteenth- and seventeenth-
century music even though a representational aesthetic drawing on
the ancient theory of *mimesis* had already taken hold in the madrigal, as it was later to do in monody and the concerto. This notion
took the form of a musical poetics based on genre as the substantive
feature of music, 'genre' here meaning nothing but a fixed relation

between the end that music was intended to serve and the technical means considered appropriate to that end. (The *prima prattica* was an ecclesiastical style, the *seconda prattica* an operatic one.) Seen in these terms, music history divides into a history of institutions on the one hand and a history of technique on the other; and an approach that draws heavily on *Verstehen* may not be utterly wide of the mark, but neither will it hit anything of significance. For it is not individual works and the composers' intentions preserved and manifest within them and subject to reconstruction by the methods of *Verstehen* that have been passed down to us and thus constitute history, so much as a nexus of generical rules through which composers sought to prove their ingenuity, though not by breaking but by fulfilling them. To put it bluntly, music history took the form not of a continual progression from work to work but of a propagation of norms – norms that regulated the balance between functions served and techniques employed.

The 'end versus means' relation characteristic of the functional concept of music gave away, in the theory of imitation, to a relation between object and likeness as constituting music's primary structure. This 'representational' view of music first came to the fore in progressive genres such as the madrigal; later it even found its way into tradition-bound genres such as church music (Bach's cantatas do not entirely fit under the rubric of functional music). Auditory creations were representations of something else; and the distinctions between tone painting, allegory and the portrayal of affections that were exaggerated to the verge of antithesis in the eighteenth century (even a figure such as 'hypotyposis' covered what we now regard as a multitude of divergent phenomena) were an entirely secondary concern to an age in which the principle of *mimesis* predominated. The poetics or theory of music took its cue less from architecture than from poetry and painting. The functional aspect receded.

Still, it would be wrong to view the portrayal of affections as a form of expressiveness. Understanding a piece of music did not mean interpreting it as a biographical document, but rather reaching an agreement with the composer as to the material content and verisimilitude of his musical rendering of reality. The dialogue which the listener conducts with the composer centres on the object represented, the musical content, and not on identification with an individual expressing his personality. And any historian who wants to make good the precept that all eras must be understood in their own terms would have to base his history of eighteenth-century music on the relation between the subject matter made available to music and the various means of rendering it. He would proceed not by *Verstehen*, by trying to understand the composer's intentions, but by *Auslegung*, by explicating the material content of the music.

After the age of sensibility, representational interest in music gradually yielded to one with a personal slant. Whereas to the seventeenth and early eighteenth centuries an affection or *ethos* was an object given by nature to be captured in music, in the late eighteenth and early nineteenth centuries the composer became the subjective agency of musical expression. Explication of the material content of music was replaced by understanding the composer as an individual on the basis of a spiritual affinity. Those who portrayed affections in the spirit of the imitation aesthetic were not speaking of themselves so much as describing as aspect of reality that was intersubjective and reproducible: listeners did not seek to penetrate the inmost depths of a composer's thought as conveyed by his music so much as to pass judgment on the accuracy, or inaccuracy, of an imitation of nature. On the other hand, the 'auto-biography in notes' that so obsessed the age of romanticism and sensibility was a musical version of the paradox of having to say something that cannot be put into words – some buried meaning inaccessible to common sense and discoverable solely through spiritual identification. To be sure, the doctrine of the affections does not, strictly speaking, preclude the possibility of psychological self-portraiture on the composer's part; but it does declare it to be aesthetically irrelevant, a private matter of no concern to the public. Furthermore, the 'subject' behind the music of romanticism and sensibility is not necessarily the composer's own: it can be an aesthetic *persona*. Subjectivity sometimes pervades the objective representation of affections, and 'self-expression' is not infre-quently the expression of an imagined rather than a real self. In short, aesthetics cannot be reduced to psychology.

With regard to today's concert public it might be exaggerated to claim that the twentieth century has seen a gradual replacement of the personal view of music by a structural one. Yet this claim has some credence if we look at the poetics of contemporary composers and of those analysts who take their aesthetic stance from current attitudes towards composition. In place of the terms 'essence' and 'image', with their Platonic or Neoplatonic overtones, that used to underlie the metaphysic of the artist, the sober Aristotelian con-cepts of 'form' and 'material' have now been put stage centre in current theories of art. In the nineteenth century the relation between material and form was a secondary factor and was taken for granted. Today it has been elevated to the primary object of aesthetic and historiological reflection. The 'propensity of the material' that Adorno proclaimed as the key category for music histories written from a twentieth-century state of awareness is no more than the same 'form versus material' relation recast in materialist terms. In our century it is no longer *Verstehen* (i.e. recognising the meaning of the auditory phenomenon as residing solely in the expression and self-portraiture of the subjective agency behind it) but structural analysis that is expected to give insight into the *raison d'être* of music. Even a public that understands nothing about structural analysis still respects its authority: better to spurn the music itself than to cast suspicion on the methods of its dissemination. The validity of whatever connections an analyst discovers does not depend on their having been consciously intended by the composer. The deciding factor is the text that the composer has produced, not the intentions behind it. The individual is the function of his creation, and not, as in the nineteenth century, the other way round.

Explanation, explication, understanding, analysis: explaining a work on the basis of the norms of the genre that it represents; explicating the material content embodied in the work; understanding the composer behind the work; and analysing the connections that bind the various parts of a work into a text. These methods correspond to the different principles that, for the past half-millennium that we call the modern age, have given music its meaning and established it as an art form. These principles, it must be repeated, are not mutually exclusive, but replaced each other as the prevailing view of their respective ages. The fact that the nineteenth century accorded special emphasis to the personal element, to understanding the composer, is not to say that the generic function of a work, the density of its structure, or its representational and programmatic significance were immaterial; but it does mean that the actual 'poetic' element of music, that quality by which music stands or falls as an art form, was sought in the originality with which a composer expressed his own thought and being, thereby proving himself equal to the paradoxical task of making us sense the indescribable and ineffable.

So the *Verstehen* method owes its privileged position over competing approaches to the fact that historicism is imprisoned by the particular assumptions of its age. But we should not let this insight into the historical limitations of this method carry us away into maintaining that the theory of *Verstehen* as developed in the last century is now a useless piece of tradition that can safely be disregarded in modern theories of history. True, it is hardly possible to adopt the solutions arrived at in the philosophy of history without intellectual misgivings. Yet the question of how we can understand a person other than ourselves at all will retain its urgency in the aesthetics and history of music as long as classical and romantic music, both of which include originality and personal expression among their premises, continue to enjoy their as yet uncontested supremacy in the writing of music history and in musical performance.

Reflections on *Verstehen* in history typically try to steer a course between the Scylla of rational norms codified in the abstract and the Charybdis of intangible irrationality. Nineteenth-century historiologists or historical theorists sought an authority or point of reference somewhere beyond the discarded idea of universal and equable rationality and a not entirely trustworthy form of intuition, which had nothing more substantial to legitimate it than intimations of spiritual kinship.

It is a necessary condition for any understanding of a thing that there exist within the person who attains the understanding an *analogon* of that which is to be understood, an inborn, prefigurative concord between subject and object. Understanding does not simply originate from the former, nor is it merely inferred from the latter: it is both at once . . . To understand oneself one must have understood oneself in another sense beforehand. In history, this precursory foundation to understanding is especially clear, for all things that effect world history also take place within the human mind.

Thus, according to Wilhelm von Humboldt in 'Über die Aufgabe des Geschichtsschreibers', the subject–object distinction is suspended in the case of historical *Verstehen* insofar as the subject that reaches the understanding sees itself reflected in the historical agent; for it is the historical agent, provided he is an 'agent' in the strong sense and not a mere ancillary figure, that has elicited the rational dimension of history reconstructed by the historian. Humboldt deliberately avoids the opposing radical views that reason has no basis in history and that history is non-rational. Instead, he has taken reason – not a pre-existent, well-defined sort of reason but one produced by and still in a state of evolutionary flux – and anchored it in history so that knowledge of history comes to mean knowledge of oneself, of human rationality in action. Rationality does not reign supreme in history as an abstract norm and arbiter.

But neither is it, in its instrumental or pragmatic aspect, a mere tool of human self-assertion in a history whose progress, seen as a whole, is hopelessly irrational. According to Hegel,

In our language 'history' combines both the objective and the subjective meanings of the term, referring equally to the *historiam rerum gestarum* and to the *res gestas* themselves . . . We should view this combination of the two meanings as of a higher order than mere external coincidence: it is responsible for the fact that historical records appear simultaneously with the actual historical deeds and events. There is a common substance inherent in each which leads to their being produced at one and the same time . . . Those periods, be they centuries or millennia, which the peoples of the world experienced before the advent of written history and which may well have been replete with their revolutions, mass migrations and upheavals of the most tumultuous sort, nevertheless have no history in the objective sense as they have left behind no history in the subjective sense – no historical records (*Die Vernunft in der Geschichte*, pp. 144–6).

History does not exist apart from our awareness of it, and written history is itself historical fact. Hegel's thesis sounds strangely obsolete in an age of archaeological histories based on artifacts rather than records. However, it was not Hegel's intention to disparage those nations and peoples that had no 'history' but rather to determine what we are justified in calling history at all, as opposed to mere chance occurrence. Furthermore, leaving metaphysics for methodology, the provocative thought that 'things happen rationally in world history' – a thought that was a *bête noire* to sceptical historians such as Burckhardt – expresses a precondition for the fact that history can not only be chronicled or made the object of irrational empathy or aesthetic contemplation, but also be known. This is not to say that everything that has ever happened has been rational, merely that there can be no talk of history taking place where rationality has yet to appear. And rationality includes reflecting on rationality itself, just as historical awareness belongs to history.

We understand even the most remote of things, allowing that they have a common origin, by, as we call it, projecting ourselves . . . not, of course, to the limits of our individual personalities, but in a certain general manner. For it is not our empirical ego *per se* that is capable of being thus transported so far beyond its original confines, but solely the essential and lasting rather than the ephemeral part of that ego . . . The richer our empirical ego, i.e. the greater the plenitude of its experiences from all walks of life, the more well appointed will seem the general ego within it (Droysen, *Texte zur Geschichtstheorie*, p. 14).

These lines might cause some raising of eyebrows. For the belief that anyone can understand anyone else, and judge and counsel him, is evidently a European prejudice resulting from a lack of sufficient humility toward the strange and alien, a prejudice that underpinned, and was in turn partly consolidated by, historicism. However, we must bear in mind that the 'general ego' that Droysen refers to is nothing immediate and pre-existing – no inviolable common essence or residuum left behind after all historical, ethnic and social differences have been extracted – but something that must be acquired. The 'general' ego that is 'richer' than the 'empirical' one arises through a process of refinement, not by reduction to a 'common sense' of the sort all too often posited by the historically naive.[1] Nor is the *Verstehen* principle, as Droysen conceived it, meant to imply that all manifestations of human volition are equally comprehensible, i.e. can be related to an internal agency accessible to us by reason of its similarity to our own mental structure. Droysen, whom no-one could accuse of being naive, was fully aware of the resistance offered by many phenomena to the probings of the historian. Rather, he intended his principle to mean that if history is to aspire to more than the mere compilation of dates it must be based on the assumption that what we do and what we create can be understood in principle, even if many of our deeds and creations remain incomprehensible in particular instances. The 'general ego' is an anthropological hypothesis made in support of a methodological postulate; feeling compelled to broach the subject of history's conditions of possibility, Droysen sought refuge in his 'walks of life' metaphysic.

We have seen how inferences are drawn from human deeds or creations about the inner agency which they 'externalise', thus becoming comprehensible to us. This view was given a new twist at the hands of Schleiermacher and his later disciple Dilthey in the form of *Lebensphilosophie*. Here a text is said to express a *Lebensmoment*, or roughly a 'slice of life'; and this *Lebensmoment*, which has received its outward expression in the text, must in turn be seen as part of a large whole called a *Lebenszusammenhang*, a coherent and self-contained 'life context'. For these two thinkers the biographical method that dominated nineteenth-century music historio-

---

[1] *Translator's note:* 'Common sense' is used here in its philosophical meaning, i.e. those truths and convictions given by nature and hence held in common by all men.

graphy was a direct consequence of the hermeneutic precept that all things individual and particular – works and deeds no less than sentences in a text – must be interpreted in terms of the larger context from which they originated and within which they served their separate functions. Hence, once a musical creation comes under the influence of hermeneutics, where it is seen to be an externalisation of a *Lebensmoment*, which is in turn part of a *Lebenszusammenhang*, it is not left in aesthetic isolation but becomes a fragment from a 'life work'. On the other hand, the turn to *Lebensphilosophie* gives evidence of an effort to go beyond the *ergon* or completed work to the *energeia* concealed within it. The creation is meant to be dissolved, as it were, and restored to the elements whence it came. And mistrustful as the *Zeitgeist* has been in recent decades of that sort of historical intuition that claims spiritual affinity but acts on whim, it nevertheless still remains current practice to revert from the hard reality of the completed work to the possibilities that once were open to the composer, from the received form to its genesis, and from concrete texts to hidden psychological states or dispositions of the unconscious. Historians may not talk about *Lebensphilosophie*, but they practise it nonetheless.

Dilthey based his analysis of *Verstehen* in history on the concept of *Erlebnis* ('experience'). This quite sober and unemphatic category had as its object, first and foremost, the simple truth that, in the natural sciences, the immediate day-to-day experiences of ordinary existence are traced back to hypothetical constructs – to relations between space and time, mass and motion – and that a complementary science is conceivable which would take the opposite approach and comprehend experiences within the living context to which they belonged before being seized upon by the analytical methods of the natural sciences. It was this return from *Erlebnis* to *Leben*, from experience to life, that Dilthey called *Verstehen*. And yet the 'life' that endows experiences with meaning and thereby makes them comprehensible bears the marks of time. Anthropology resolves into history. Hence it would be wrong to take *Verstehen*, as Dilthey conceived it, to be a mystical process, an immediate and intuitive perception of the essence of life. Rather, it is a means of using historical thought to grasp that meaning that attaches to a 'slice of life' by virtue of its being part of a 'life context'. Hermeneutics derives ultimately from textual criticism, not mysticism.

Obsolete as it may seem, a controversy over *Verstehen* versus *Erklären* ('understanding' versus 'explanation') still figures in current discussions between historians and sociologists on intentional, causal and functional interpretations. Yet polemical zeal combined with a want of proper background reading has led to misconceptions that not infrequently reduce this discussion to the level of a mock dialogue. A typical instance is the misuse of the categories 'nomothetic' and 'idiographic' proposed by Wilhelm Windelband in 1894. True, Windelband assumed that the aim of history was to depict and elucidate events and situations that can never be repeated. Yet he in no way implied that hypothetical laws of sociology, psychology or economics were to be left out of historical explanations altogether. Not only that, it is flagrantly wrong to use Windelband's categories to claim for a particular fact – a musical one, for instance – that one method or another enjoys, *a priori*, special prerogatives. Whether a particular phenomenon belongs to a nomothetic or an idiographic discipline does not depend upon the concrete fact as such but on the historian's interests and aims. As Windelband put it in 'Geschichte und Naturwissenschaft', 'The difference between natural science and history does not set in until we come to the utilisation of facts to obtain knowledge.' Hence this difference is not ontological but methodological.

Heinrich Rickert took the ideas of Windelband one step further to expound the thesis that the 'cultural sciences', by which he meant the historical and philosophical disciplines, examine the nature of things 'insofar as they are conditioned by values'.[2] Now the word 'value' – which, especially in the plural, rings strangely hollow nowadays – may puzzle methodologists who still cling to the 'value-free' principle of Max Weber. Yet it should not be taken to mean that the historian himself assigns values in order to structure the history he is writing, but rather that he describes objects part of whose meaning consists in their having a bearing to values. Deprived of such value-relations, the facts that make up the material of history would be no more than debris, a choatic and amorphous mass left behind by the past. These values, however, which are the *sine qua non* for turning the confusion of events and situations into coherent narrative history, are not devised by the historian and applied to history from without. On the contrary, they are lit upon or discovered within history itself. The value structure that makes possible a *historia rerum gestarum* is prefigured in the *res gestae* themselves (though the distinction between value-judgments as objects and as the premises of historiography is not so clear in

2 *Kulturwissenschaft und Naturwissenschaft*, p. 78.

scholarly practice as Rickert proclaims it to be in theory: construct merges with reconstruction).

According to Max Weber, human actions, and by analogy the production of human creations, are modes of behaviour linked with a subjective meaning. And it is the task of the historian to reconstruct the pattern of meanings behind past actions. Yet no-one would maintain that human actions are conditioned exclusively by intentionality; they are equally dependent on conditions that have causal or functional explanations. The sole point of contention is whether, and if so to what extent, the structures that accommodate intentional actions should be merely touched upon in passing or placed stage centre and elevated as the fundamental object of historical inquiry. It is not the dialectics of events and structures, i.e. the obvious fact that actions take place within institutions and institutions are compounded of actions, that traditional and social historians are at odds about. Rather, the question is whether the emphasis should fall on the individual processes from which the system ultimately derives, or on the system that takes shape as a result of these processes.

Intentional interpretations depict conscious motives and objectives, and as such represent 'intrinsic' explanations. Causal or functional interpretations, on the other hand, being reconstructions of economic or social mechanisms that virtually always remain unconscious, are 'extrinsic'. (Functional interpretations differ from causal ones in that they merely establish a correlation between two given states of affairs, say a psychological and a sociological one, without determining which is the basis and cause of the other.) Claiming *a priori* precedence for one of these two methods in order to discredit the other as unconvincing or immaterial would be dogmatic and nonsensical. Yet it is equally wrong to seek comfort in the trite Solomonian judgment that we are at perfect liberty to switch 'intrinsic' and 'extrinsic' approaches according to our interests in view. It would be more appropriate to ask how subtle and to the point, or crude and irrelevant, are the statements made about musical phenomena using the one or the other method. Nor is there any need to feel powerless in face of the theoretical argument that the object under investigation only becomes such by virtue of the method chosen, i.e. that to a generalising social historian music means something quite different from what it means to the traditional historian with his individualist approach. The fact is that there exists a basic core of material belonging to music on which any method must prove its worth. A dispute, for example, between

an historian who restricts 'twentieth-century' music solely to esoteric contemporary works which he then tries to decipher by analysing their intrinsic structure, and a sociologist who first proclaims
that only those musical phenomena that reach a mass public are
relevant to history and then proceeds to subject them to a 'nomothetic' study – such a dispute may well be conceivable as part of an
intellectual exercise, as a mock dialogue in which neither side
listens to the other. But it little alters the prevailing tacit understanding that no music history that ignores the problem of these
two opposing realms stands a chance of doing justice to its subject.

Thus it would seem that 'intrinsic' historical understanding and
'extrinsic' observation, i.e. the interpretation of intentions and the
explanation of causes or functions, may exist in a thoroughly complementary relation to one another, a relation characterised by
mutual tolerance or even mutual support. Yet this relation blurs
and turns into distrust the moment the postulate is raised that we
must understand past ages in their own terms lest we construe them
anachronistically rather than historically.[3]

A resolution to this controversy that would avoid piecemeal
reconciliation and return to basic principles is scarcely imaginable
now or in the immediate future. For one, it would be patently
absurd to take, say, the opinions of Enlightenment thinkers on the
illusory nature of magic or the convictions of modern physicists that
the ideal numbers of the Platonists and Pythagoreans are flimsy
metaphysical constructs, and use them as a basis for historical judgments on the musical cultures of Antiquity. Conversely, it is no
easy matter, when looking at a fabric of historical argument, to
pluck out the more recently acquired insights because the ages
being studied knew nothing about them. There is little point in
writing, for example, a history of music theory without resorting to
the more recent arguments, developed only in our own century,
that cast doubt on the 'physicalism' of eighteenth- and nineteenth-
century accounts of harmony, for it was these very arguments that
challenged historians to turn from an 'intrinsic' historical and theoretical explanation to an 'extrinsic' sociological one in order to
illuminate the curious dependence of harmony at that time on an
imperfect understanding of the natural sciences.

Furthermore, it remains unclear just where we should draw the
bounds within which we may criticise a past view in terms of its own

[3] It is an irony seldom noticed by the historians who commit it that while past epochs
may be interpreted in their own terms, the present is generally derived from, and
explained in terms of, the past.

age without running the risk of being accused of anachronism and wilfulness. Is it legitimate or not to criticise the belief, held by many music theorists as late as the eighteenth century, that a number is an active principle and the simplicity of a ratio constitutes physical grounds for the striking effect of a consonance, as not merely wayward but historically inappropriate, considering the state of knowledge and methodology attained at that time in the natural sciences? Where, in the muddle of competing and often in-compatible opinions of an age, is the 'real' spirit of the times to be found? Which level of awareness is the prevailing one and should be used by historians to characterise the age: the most progressive one, the one most widely disseminated, or the one belonging to the socially and politically influential figures of the day? And is it the historian's business to take sides with those groups who determined the afterlife of an age in the eyes of history by dictating what was to be written at the time?

The problems, it would seem, are labyrinthine and virtually inex-tricable. There is little an historian can do to avoid falling victim to them other than take them up as a topic.

7

The value-judgment: object or premise of history?

Historians, according to their philosopher critics, are inescapably embroiled in a contradiction which can be summed up roughly in the following formula: an historian's need to rely on subjective judg-ments stands in direct proportion to the degree of objectivity he seeks in his history. However dispassionately and impartially he tries to reconstruct 'the way it really was', he is nonetheless compelled to distinguish between essential things that 'belong to history' and in-essential things that can safely be disregarded. And he does this on the basis of criteria which are thoroughly subjective, being rooted in his own background and social position, in his beliefs and experi-ences. Nor does positing a collective rather than an individual sub-ject for written history substantially affect this problem.

Yet these philosophical doubts as to the notion of objectivity in history are cast in terms that vary between two extremes. One is undisguised ill-will and resentment; the other is a subtle scepticism which defers matters to a final arbiter. This scepticism, however, at least admits the possibility that history can withstand what Jürgen Habermas has called the dialectics of 'knowledge and interest' – i.e. the difficulty that an ineradicably subjective element is apparently both a condition for and a barrier to historical insight – by subjecting them to a continuing process of reflection. Historians can keep the problem at bay, as it were, by probing it with ever greater refinement.

Now, as anyone who can distinguish between objectivity and mere blindness to the problems at hand will agree, deciding upon a topic, choosing a point of view and selecting materials are all bound up with interests that are firmly rooted in the way the historian conducts his life. Yet it does not follow that any pronouncement on history can be reduced completely and utterly to an underlying dogma riddled with particular interests. For whether an historical presentation can rank as scholarly or not depends less upon the values which it takes as its starting point than upon the methods used to connect facts in a field whose very bounds are marked out by value-relations.

The crudest and hence most popular form of ideological critique consists of mechanically casting aspersions on historical judgments by accusing the historian of belonging to a social group that is totally incapable of ever discerning 'the way it really was'. Anyone with reactionary views would thus forfeit *a priori* the possibility of understanding history, of using thought to master it. Zealots who feel confidence and satisfaction in the thought that they are in possession of the undivided truth measure the validity or fallibility of a scholarly proposition against nothing more substantial than the opinions of the person who voiced it, insisting that knowledge is whatever happens to tally with the slogans of their own self-styled 'objective and universal' party instead of allowing the possibility that new knowledge might, in fact, actually further their own interests.

In answer to this brutalised form of ideological critique we should pose the distinction – by now somewhat threadbare, but still sufficient for our purposes – between genesis and validity, i.e. between the origins of a thing and its essence. The fact that an argument has resulted from ill-will does not necessarily discredit that argument and mean that it can safely be cast aside with a slighting reference to its humble birth. (The high-minded belief that true understanding can only come from sympathy is an idealistic prejudice that has been obsolete at least since Nietzsche.) Reconstructing the conditions under which a proposition came into being will never suffice to establish whether or not it is valid. And an historical study based on apparently questionable value-relations – for instance a history of nineteenth-century music that takes the idea of nationalism as a criterion for separating the essential from the inessential – can nevertheless achieve insights that are 'objective' to the extent that they are sufficiently in accord, firstly, with the material whose internal cohesion is meant to be reconstructed and, secondly, with the current state of knowledge that the study is meant to build upon.

There seems to be no reconciling Marxists and non-Marxists in the controversy over partisanship, the less so as they often do not even try to understand each other. If we are to avoid a mock dialogue in which both sides talk and neither listens, we should at least be allowed to assume agreement on the point that historical knowledge always builds upon non-scholarly interests (though without necessarily remaining bound to them in the course of the investigation) and that these interests make themselves felt in the statement of the problem to be investigated and in the choice of material to be considered 'relevant'. Objectivity will be forever beyond the reach of those who believe that historical facts speak for themselves without first being made articulate by questions involving some measure of subjectivity on the part of the historian, i.e. those who believe that the historian merely notes down things which appear at first blush to be facts. Holders of this view are simply being naive, which is as much as saying that they are biassed without knowing it.

If we want to make this methodological dispute useful to the theory of science rather than having it peter out in an exchange of ideological slogans we must begin by deciding in favour of one of the consequences to be drawn from Habermas's dialectics of 'knowledge and human interests'. In a rational discussion, the claim that an historian is holding to the notions of objectivity and impartiality means no more than that he has made his own interests and his own partiality themselves the object of historical reflection. (For history, like philosophy, is by nature a self-reflecting discipline that can use the tools at its disposal to objectify and study its own premises.) And the aim of this reflection is to make explicit, and in so doing to minimise, the influence of any subjective elements, whether personal or collective. However, the degree to which objectivity can be reached, and the extent to which an historian should strive for it at all without relegating himself to the sterile function of merely registering facts, cannot be determined by reference to fixed standards. It must simply be left to our sense of what is fitting and appropriate. All that we know for certain is that whatever precision it is within our powers to attain will never be reached by leaving ourselves, the observers, out of the picture, but solely by making the observer's position an integral part of the agreement reached on the cognitive process chosen and the results obtained, and by learning to appreciate just how far the influence of this position extends.

The opposite consequence of the inseparability of knowledge and interest – one that is puzzling to non-Marxists – is the Marxists' determination to ensconce themselves, as it were, in their own partisanship, having previously made themselves aware of its assumptions and implications by subjecting it to historical reflection just as do non-Marxist historians. This is tantamount to singling out and taking to extremes a dependence which they can never entirely escape in any case. Yet it is not enough simply to accuse Marxist historians of shunning objectivity altogether, for the sole reason that it is only partially attainable at best. The point is that Marxists consider their histories objective precisely by virtue of their being partisan, since the cause they espouse happens to be enacting the dictates of Marx's 'law of motion in history'.

This apology for partisanship in history has an emotional appeal that still makes it attractive; but it is an obvious instance of circular argument, and not one that lends itself to vindication as a hermeneutic circle. The Marxist historian must know his historical truths in advance, before beginning his work. Otherwise he can never be certain that the partisan approach he has taken will coincide with the objectivity that he can attain by it. Seen in this light, his work never proceeds beyond the subsidiary activity of tracing and adding details to what is at least in all fundamental respects already present, in the consciousness of the class whose political practices are meant to represent historical truth, or to have that truth on their side. Marxist polemics against non-Marxists work both ways. First and foremost, the Marxists deny the claim of non-Marxist theorists of history that detachment from interests is possible at all. Yet far from saying that we *cannot* rise above our prejudices, what they actually mean is that we *should not* rise above them.

In sharp contrast to the Marxists, who maintain that theory reaches the highest attainable degree of truth by interaction with practice – meaning a particular kind of practice – non-Marxist theorists of history cling to the exactly opposite belief and hold that it is detachment from practice that opens up the possibility of at least approaching objectivity. This form of objectivity is realistic rather than abstract and utopian; it has been given the operational definition of 'intersubjectivity', and is expected to rectify the subjective biasses of the individual historian. Intersubjectivity consists in agreement being reached within the so-called 'scientific community', one of whose constituent properties is its exemption from the immediate cares of political and economic practice.

Max Weber kindled a dispute over 'value-judgments' which has spread from sociology into history. This dispute hinges primarily (with the exception of those controversies arising from misconceptions) on the question of whether Weber's distinction between 'valuation' and 'value-relation' is sufficient to keep normative dogma from creeping into a science that is supposed to proceed along strictly empirical lines, and at the same time to prevent historical material from collapsing into a chaos of facts in which the historian draws connections from sheer personal preference with no obligation to compel conviction. A 'value-relation' is devised or reconstructed by the historian in order to winnow the essential and characteristic facts of a past era from the insignificant or incidental ones. It differs from a 'valuation' insofar as the one represents an objective norm whose validity is established by the historian, whereas the other is a subjective norm with which the historian himself is in sympathy. For example: the history of late-eighteenth- and nineteenth-century music is unintelligible without some reference to the originality postulate, whereby self-expression and technical innovation were expected of composers of artificial music; yet the historian who accepts this is in no way obliged to adopt the aesthetic as his own and apply it in his attempts to come to terms with his own musical environment. On the contrary, the historian recognises the existence of a 'value-relation' without necessarily having to share the 'valuation' that it contains – although, of course, he is perfectly at liberty to accept it if he so wishes.

Still, there is a small difficulty. The historian actually 'finds' only a small percentage of the value-relations that guide him in his account of a past age. The rest he must 'produce'. True, these value-relations must pass the muster of empiricism if they are not simply to remain arbitrary articles of faith. For example, the thesis that developments in nineteenth-century music can largely be accounted for by the efforts to cultivate the speech character of music stands a good chance of ordering the historical facts into a pattern that would illuminate without being superficial – and this despite the fact that the prevailing aesthetics of the times turned on the concept of 'beauty in music' and the conflict between absolute and programmatic music. Yet the day-to-day practice of scholarship goes to show, firstly, that 'the facts' have a habit of adapting themselves with equal readiness to conflicting value-relations, and, secondly, that the value-relations that the historian devises for a particular segment of the past and the valuations that he himself believes in, though separable in theory, are in fact closely related both psychologically and in scholarly practice, for the simple reason that 'the facts of history', as mentioned above, will put up with various, even incompatible, value-relations with astonishing indifference (particularly as 'valuations' inevitably play a role in decisions as to which facts are 'historical' and 'belong to history' in the first place).

Seen in this light, Max Weber's distinction gives us less cause for relief than grounds for disquiet. So as not to become muddled and wearied by the tortuous and at times pained controversies over 'valuations' and 'value-relations' we should recall that history is a self-reflecting discipline that can make its own underlying assumptions the object of further investigation which, being historical in its own right, does not exceed the bounds of its own discipline.

The trivial pronouncement that Wagner's *Ring* is one of the outstanding works of the nineteenth century can be substantiated in terms of the history of its reception, with no mention of aesthetic norms being necessary. In other words, the thesis is verifiable by empirical means. In contrast, the claim that Wagner's tetralogy represents the historical realisation of the ideal of music drama – an ideal which had arisen time and again in the course of operatic history, only to be forgotten – harbours normative premises that no-one, it would seem, is obliged to share. Yet the historian's decision to accept or reject these premises need not be merely arbitrary; the manner in which this alleged norm falls into place within the larger history of the ideals of music theatre can be studied empirically, using the means of history, not aesthetics. And, with some stretch of the imagination, the result of such an investigation might even show that our judgment of the *Ring* is sufficiently compatible with the notions of operatic aesthetics prevalent in nineteenth-century Germany to warrant being called a representative expression of a 'value-relation' which the historian of German opera can then draw upon without leaving himself open to accusations of blind prejudice. Finally, the 'value-relation' whose significance to history the historian is trying to ascertain can itself be subjected to a process of 'valuation', on a fourth level of reflection, using premises that the historian himself believes in.

Value-judgments must, of course, be kept logically separate from factual judgments; but this does not exclude the fact that, in practical terms, value-judgments are quite often partly grounded on factual ones, and conversely factual judgments are often influenced by value-judgments. Even asseverations of causality can be dependent on moral and aesthetic convictions, however dubious this might seem to a philosopher of science. We might ask whether the 'cause' of the collapse of traditional tonality around 1910 – at least in that part of artificial music which, in retrospect, proved to have the greatest historical significance – lay in the 'depletion' of the system or in the 'aggression' of a few composers. But clearly this could never be decided without passing judgment as to whether it is in keeping with the nature of music to extend musical logic and expression as far as is humanly possible, or whether it would be more 'reasonable' for the sake of intelligibility not to abandon an institution which, though partly undermined, is nevertheless still viable.

This, however, is not to say that the moral and aesthetic judgments which the historian unexpectedly finds himself having to resort to are beyond the pale of rational discussion. Above all we should bear in mind that even if normative articles of faith cannot logically be derived from facts they are still empirically subject to their influence. The distinction in theory between normative and descriptive statements sometimes blinds us to the fact that, in daily life, value-decisions are constantly being rectified on the basis of the facts that come our way. Once we concede this interaction of norms and facts, we even find it legitimate for an historian to do more than meekly accept earlier norms as valid for their time and social group, and instead to size them up against the knowledge which was available to the age in question and might conceivably have exercised a corrective influence.

The 'value-relations' discovered by an historian in the music and musical culture of earlier periods and the 'valuations' that he himself is disposed to make have always been transmitted side by side as part of tradition, the survival of the past in the present. We never make completely unpreconceived judgments in an immediate and primary relationship to an object, but are always assimilating or rejecting received opinion, whether consciously or unconsciously. To put it bluntly, judgments are made with reference less to actual things than to earlier judgments.

Granted that 'valuations' and 'value-relations' have a mediator in tradition, it then becomes clear that the problem of selecting what 'belongs to history', i.e. of distinguishing the essential from the inessential among the things that confront the historian in his daily rounds, is conspicuously distinct from that dilemma that historical theorisers have construed as the bane of historians. History's philosopher critics see the historian as inextricably entangled in a dialectical process of having to make value-decisions on an utterly subjective basis so as to turn a chaos of facts into narrative history, of having to 'subjectify' his judgments in order to 'objectify' the diffuse matter of history into manageable form. Yet these critics base their reflections on a view of the historian's craft that is gravely suspect.

Music history deals with a canon of musical works which historians concede as 'belonging to history', not in the weak sense of merely having once existed and exercised an influence, but in the strong sense of towering above the debris otherwise left behind by the past. This 'History' which a work may or may not belong to is not merely the sum total of everything that has ever existed or taken place – a sum that would in any case be impossible to calculate. Rather it is a distillation of that part of tradition which the present considers relevant or essential to itself, whether from curiosity about its own past or from the opposing urge to gain self-detachment by assimilating the alien and remote.

Yet the notion of a musical canon has its ambiguities. So as not to become confused and fall victim to fallacies we must, to coin a phrase, distinguish between the canon *chosen* and the canon *chosen from*. Many music historians are attracted less to Handel, Haydn, Mendelssohn or Stravinsky than to Bach, Beethoven, Schumann or Schoenberg; yet however much these predilections may influence their choice of topic or find expression in the aesthetic judgments scattered through their writings, they little alter the canon upon which the writing of music history, even by those hostile to Handel or Stravinsky, is based. A music historian who does not feel the remotest affinity with Gluck's music and is rather predisposed to agree with Handel's ill-tempered opinion of him will nonetheless scarcely intend the composer of *Orpheus* and *Iphigenia in Tauris* to be excluded from or consigned to the periphery of music history as he understands it. The canon that he decides upon for aesthetic reasons, i.e. his subjective selection, leaves virtually unchanged the larger canon from which his choice must inevitably be made. And it is this primary, pre-existent canon rather than the second-ary, subjective one that represents a premise of music historiogra-phy.

This distinction can be refined still further. Even a 'value-rel-ation' that leads to a thoroughly onesided selection of facts does not in principle jeopardise the scholarly nature of an historical nar-rative. There is nothing to prevent an historian from picking works from operative history and combining them so as to reveal the basis of their formal principles in music drama, so long as he does not claim that this approach embraces the 'whole' or the 'single most essential aspect' of opera history. Onesidedness is not irreconcil-able with objectivity. Still, an opera historian who has taken his critical bearings from Wagner runs no small risk of letting silence about Rossini turn into unwarranted disparagement, i.e. of unin-tentionally confusing an objective 'value-relation' that imparts form to historical matter with a subjective 'valuation' that is his own private affair.

Attempts to probe the canon of musical works have generally proceeded from a distinction between aesthetic and historical cri-teria. Aesthetic standing takes the form of a quality that attaches to a work in its own right. Historical significance, on the other hand, refers to a role played within a context: a work may be a particu-larly telling expression of the 'spirit of the age', a decisive step in the evolution of a genre, form or particular technique, or a founda-tion and starting point for works which, on their own merits, have been accepted for display in the imaginary museum of music history. The fact that a work has 'gone down in history', as the phrase goes, can be justified either directly on the basis of what it is, or indirectly by virtue of what it foreshadows or alludes to.

However, the concept of historical import is ambiguous and mis-leading. It can refer either to effects in space and time which can be measured, or at least estimated, or to the fact that particular works or other historical facts have been endowed with symptomatic significance within a structural context or 'ideal type' devised by the historian. The far-reaching influence once exercised by Stamitz's symphonies constitutes, to use Max Weber's phrase, 'material grounds' for accepting these works into music history regardless of what we feel their artistic value to be. The programme of a musical soirée attended by Herr von Uffenbach during his sojourn in Paris in 1715, however, belongs to history only to the extent that it reflects the structure of early-eighteenth-century concert life. Within the notion of historical significance a distinction must be drawn between a work's having an 'impact' and its being a 'symptom' or what Max Weber called a 'cognitive vehicle'.

Whether or not a piece of music proves to be of historical significance depends in large part, if not exclusively, on the point of view chosen by the historian and on the problems that he is trying to solve. Yet these problems are in turn subject to a pronouncement as to their 'relevance' or 'irrelevance'; and this pronouncement is, in the final analysis, normative, though tempered in scholarly practice by empirical factors.

The general run of things that historians have to deal with usually falls somewhere between the two aforementioned extremes, i.e. between historical impact, which is clearly discernible, and symptomatic importance, which accrues to an otherwise unlikely fact with the devising of an 'ideal type'. If, for instance, we wish to assess the part played by *Rienzi* in the history of grand opera, it is just as inadequate to recount its rather uneventful later history as it is to analyse the work as symptomatic of certain structural features of the species 'grand opera'. Instead, the outcome depends essentially upon our larger view of history, i.e. whether we treat the genres 'music drama' and 'grand opera' as separate and distinct, or as closely related parallel developments. In the first instance, *Rienzi* becomes an outgrown preliminary stage on the path to music drama, and hence a document more of biographical than of historiographical significance; in the second, it offers revealing evidence of a connection between the two genres that is fundamental both aesthetically and historically.

Once the questions that mark the limits of a study have been posed, the answers contained in or prefigured by the historical facts can be recorded with a degree of objectivity (meaning relevance to the matter at hand and intersubjective validity) that is not so far removed from the standards of the exact sciences as many historians have let themselves be intimidated by physics into believing. Therefore, when criticising the alleged historical significance of certain facts, we should first turn to the questions posed by the historian before addressing ourselves to his answers. For example, the historical role we accord to J. C. F. Fischer depends entirely on how significant we feel the notion of fugue cycles arranged by key to be in the development of the fugue and the history of tonality. If we conclude – *The Well-Tempered Clavier* notwithstanding – that the cyclic principle is incidental to the aesthetics and history of the fugue and that, in the evolution of tonality, the point is the range and variety of keys not between pieces but within a single piece, then the *Ariadne musica* as history turns into the trifle that it always has been as a work of art.

It would be abstract and high-handed to make a radical distinction between aesthetic and historical criteria, between what a piece of music is in its own right and what it becomes as part of an historical context. To begin with, many aesthetic categories also include historical elements: the notions of novelty and originality, or epigonism and trivialisation, can to all intents and purposes be said to owe their use in the theory of art to a transformation of historical judgments into aesthetic ones. (The originality postulate is the hallmark of aesthetics in the age of historical awareness.) Secondly, not only the aesthetic judgments themselves, but the criteria they derive from, are subject to historical change: it would be a misleading anachronism to speak of epigonism in sixteenth-century music, no matter how much the production of motets at the end of the century seems to cry out for this label. A stylistic imitation that would have been considered a mark of weakness in the nineteenth century may well have betokened piety in the sixteenth, a willingness on the composer's part to trust in established tradition rather than expose himself to the dangers of developing his own 'manner'.

Nevertheless, the distinction between historical and aesthetic significance is by no means useless; we must only bear in mind that it is vague and provisional, and try less to make a hard and fast dichotomy of it than to understand the dialectics that it gives rise to. As we shall see, the canon of things 'belonging to history' is largely presented to the historian 'from without'; and, to identify this outward connection, the term 'aesthetic' as opposed to 'historical' is a quite handy label for things that must inevitably precede an historical study, even though not all the features that contribute to the establishment of a musical canon are aesthetic in nature. To the audiences of the nineteenth century, when the canon was formulated, the classical status of the composers whose music makes up the bedrock of music history – Palestrina, Bach, Handel, Gluck, Haydn, Mozart and Beethoven – did not depend exclusively on the aesthetic standing of their works. Rather, a 'classic' was always the exemplary composer, the *classicus auctor*, within a specific genre, just as in literature Sophocles was the classical

author of tragedy and Homer of the epic. To call Palestrina the
'classic' of Catholic church music and Bach of its Protestant
counterpart, Handel of the oratorio and Gluck of *opera seria*,
Haydn of the string quartet, Mozart of *opera buffa* and Beethoven
of the symphony, was to make at one and the same time an aes-
thetic-normative judgment and an historical-descriptive one: to the
nineteenth century's way of thinking, the emergence of a musical
genre meant its dependence upon a model, and the scattered facts
of history would never have settled into narrative form at all if they
had not first been brought to bear on generic norms as manifested
in paradigmatic works.

   Now, historians were not aware of the distinction between aesthetic and historical factors until long after the fact, while the
musical canon was formed on the basis of a hodge-podge of categories of the sort that characterise the notions of 'classical' and
'classicism'. This implies nothing less than that the canon had already been established before historians began to reflect upon its
significance as a framework for music history and to see the problems lurking in the relationship between the aesthetic judgments it
contained and the historiographical needs it was meant to fulfil.
The canon was originally part, not of historical, but of pre-his-
torical awareness. The concept of the 'classical' is, in a manner of
speaking, its legacy to music history, which drew sustenance from it
(an historian would be at an utter loss without at least some inkling
as to what belongs to 'History' in the first place), but at the same
time undermined it by reducing this once normative concept to a
mere label for a period, with no normative implications whatsoever.

   In sum, the canon of musical works which belong to history has
always been predetermined for the historian – at least in the first
instance and in its basic outline – either as an imaginary museum
from which he can make his subjective selection without affecting
its holdings, or as a framework that he must perforce resort to if he
wishes to write music history. A notion is still bruited about in
methodological discussions that the historian begins his work by
making a personal selection of musical works, i.e. that he first uses
his own judgment to establish a basic core of works that stand out
from the past and then weaves the works thus recognised as significant into an historical fabric. But in actual scholarly practice this
proves to be far from the case. (It almost seems as though the epi-
stemologists who triumph in discovering the naivety of straightforward empiricists are guilty of their own brand of naivety.) At the

very least it is probably impractical if not completely wrongheaded to base a theoretical discussion of the role of value-judgments in music historiography on a model that has little relevance to what historians actually do.

For an historian to 'receive' a predetermined canon – which in no way excludes the possibility of his criticising that canon – means first of all that he reconstruct 'value-relations' which have qualified works for inclusion in our imaginary museum, but also that, as an historian (and not as a listener), he adopt some of the 'valuations' handed down from the past to aid him in structuring the history that he wishes to relate. To decide that, say, Haydn's *Creation* represents one of the pillars of music history is quite different from learning the historical conditions that established the work's fame or rendered that fame possible, and also quite different from the historian's own aesthetic approbation of the work, which he is free to grant or withhold as he wishes. It is a *sui generis* case of valuation that cannot be entirely subsumed in an historical 'value-relation' reconstructed by the historian, nor in a current 'valuation' of his own devising.

As we have seen, the canon upon which music historiography is based is transmitted by tradition: historians do not compile it so much as encounter it. And the vacillation mentioned above between a 'value-relation' and a 'valuation', the former representing an object and the latter a cognitive act, is evidently characteristic of traditions. The canon is at one and the same time a bothersome impediment to, and an indispensable mainstay of, historical criticism. (If historicism were to break completely from tradition it would rob itself of its own source of sustenance.) Music historiography is incapable on its own of substantiating aesthetic judgments that allow the essential to be distinguished from the inessential; the historian needs an 'extrinsic' norm if he is not to suffocate in a chaos of facts flung together at random. (Apart from the logical impossibility of deriving normative statements from descriptive ones, it is the difference between the aesthetic and the historical sides to music, i.e. between the 'work' and the 'document', that prevents historians, lest they exceed the bounds of their discipline, from making judgments based on their own experience of a work in solitary aesthetic absorption. The historian can, indeed must, produce 'value-relations'; but it is not his business to justify 'valuations'.)

Yet music historians must make aesthetic distinctions in order to determine just what does or does not belong to history in the strong sense. The category of historical impact which, in political history, highlights the matter to be considered essential also plays a role in music history, albeit an inadequate one, since musical greatness, unlike political greatness, is possible without historical impact. Music history cannot be freed from aesthetics as politics can be freed from morality; moral strength can be just as devoid of historical impact in the political world as can aesthetic greatness. To take an example, we can hardly claim for Bach's cantatas (unlike his *Well-Tempered Clavier*) that they had an historical impact; our firm conviction of their greatness does not rest on their historical significance, which was slight (historically they might best be described as a *cul-de-sac*), but rather on an aesthetic judgment as to their inherent musical worth. We need not bother ourselves with the sophistry that musical greatness must be recognised sooner or later and that even its discovery long after the fact represents an historical impact of sorts.

Thus music history requires a pre-existent canon passed down by tradition if it is to be music history at all, i.e. a structured account of the past. Yet the fact that music history is by nature dependent on tradition does not mean that we must blindly accept what tradition has handed down to us by way of a musical canon. On the contrary, historiography and the canon it has inherited, partly as a precondition, partly as an object of study, exist in what might be described as a dialectical relation.

This has three consequences for the historian. Firstly, he can analyse the nature of, and the reasons for, the formation of the canon, i.e. he can examine the preconditions that underlie his own activity as an historian. For history, as mentioned above in a different context, is a self-reflecting discipline. The 'circle' into which it thus enters is of the hermeneutic and harmless rather than the vicious variety. Nor is the claim that an aesthetic canon will cease to be valid once its basis in history has been disclosed anything more than a dubious prejudice. It in no way weakens or invalidates a criterion to realise that it has its historical side, nor is it weak-minded epigonism on our part if we ground a norm in a tradition (not forgetting the limits of that tradition) instead of constantly invoking the imperishability of the physical world or of human nature. In the early days of the Enlightenment, as the eighteenth-century historicist movement was called, the main thrust of the derivation of norms from history was directed against their allegedly 'extratemporal' status. Since then, however, the once paradoxical and provocative contention that aesthetic norms are 'historical through and through' has shrunk to an innocuous commonplace, and the habit of clinging to the 'extratemporal' has given way to the belief that a norm is sufficiently legitimated if it can create a consensus lasting several decades.

Secondly, it would be a useful and practicable undertaking to draw attention to the categories, criteria and modes of thought (such as the idea and history of classicism) which, whether implicitly or explicitly, underlie the surviving aesthetic canon, and to contrast them with each other and arrange them in a pattern that would be no less valuable for being incomplete. Even the mere revelation that inconsistencies existed in the fabric of aesthetic categories in a given age would, when combined with an attempt to explain these inner contradictions, be quite acceptable as the result of such an effort toward systematisation. To put it as a paradox, failure here would still spell success.

Thirdly, history can influence and alter a canon of aesthetic norms either by proposing alternative norms or by unearthing historical facts that obstruct or undermine the premises of that canon. In doing this, history turns into tradition critique without exceeding its limits. History modifies the tradition it depends upon. Norms may not be derivable from facts; but this does not mean that they are impervious to the influence of facts. And impossible though it may be to use logic to compel the acceptance of norms, it is nevertheless useful, in empirical terms, to make their assumptions and consequences explicit, so as to turn sclerotic 'decisionism' into a healthy sense of proportion.

Let us take up these three consequences in order.

I

However rivetting the topic might be, no efforts have yet been made to show how and why the music-historical canon was formed, i.e. to retrace the paths that led Schütz, Gluck, Weber, Debussy and Schoenberg to a fame that seems wellnigh unassailable today. This is not to say that the gist of the problems involved has escaped us – Schütz and Protestant church music, Gluck and music drama, Weber and the 'national spirit' in music – but the heart of the matter is to be found in the details. Still, even the most cursory reflection will reveal the shallowness of the glib assumption that classical status is attained by the mere accumulation of successful performances. And complex as a comprehensive study of this sort might be, and difficult as it might be to collect material, we should have little trouble in reaching agreement on some of the points to be considered.

Firstly, a distinction must be made between success in performance, which can in principle be counted and measured even though the figures may be difficult or even impossible to obtain, and prestige, which a work can enjoy without being performed at all. Mendelssohn's discovery of the St Matthew Passion can be seen as having converted the prestige that this work already had for a select few into a successful performance: the stature of the work was never in doubt, merely the question as to whether a broad public could be convinced of what esoteric circles already knew to be the case. Even today, with the *Art of Fugue*, performances appear to be no more than ancillary demonstrations appended to a fame which was established primarily outside the bounds of musical practice and which does not need musical practice for its further propagation.

Secondly, it is a commonplace in the sociology of music that the reception of works of music must be supported by institutions if it is not to be left to chance and hence remain transitory. Pieces that fall beyond the pale of a system of institutions either remain shrouded in obscurity (as do lieder for more than one soloist), or must be adapted to existing circumstances by altering their forces (as when madrigals are performed by chorusses rather than soloists). However, institutions sustain individual works and genres in varying forms and degrees of effectiveness; and the theoretical separation of the aesthetic and institutional bases of musical fame, i.e. of its internal and external conditions, serves the merely heuristic purpose of setting categorical limits for describing those admixtures that go to make up the reality of history. The standing of Beethoven's symphonies in our concert repertory does, of course, represent a form of institutionalisation, but to a lesser extent than, and in a different sense from, the elevation of late-sixteenth-century vocal music to a paradigm for 'pure' church music, or even than the codification of Gregorian chant. The concert would never have acquired the name 'symphony concert' or taken its present form without the aesthetic demands posed by Beethoven's symphonies, which would not submit to being used, or rather abused, as prologues or epilogues to patchwork programmes, with one movement performed at the beginning of the concert and another at the end. It was the aesthetic aspect that forced a metamorphosis to take place in the institution, albeit gradually rather than immediately. The opposite applies to church music. Here the liturgical function and the style that best answered the given purpose of representing a text in music were both predetermined 'extrinsically' by the institution. Aesthetic value, while not superfluous, seems more an addition to, than a natural outgrowth of, the basic essence of this genre.

Finally, fame in music is always connected with one or more of the 'carrier strata' that coexist within a society, 'carrier stratum' being understood to mean a public whose members have something in common besides their musical interests (there would be no point in speaking of 'carrier strata' for modern or early music if the groups associated with, say, electronic music or lute music were held together as social units by nothing but their unusual tastes in music). Even during an age with a virtually unchanging social structure and a fixed conception of artificial music it is by no means always the same carrier stratum that determines whether a composer's oeuvre should be admitted to the imaginary museum or not. Anton Webern's reputation, unlike that of Richard Strauss, was established not by the concert public but in esoteric circles which, unlike the adherents of Matthias Hauer, managed to gain influence in the mass media and thus escape being condemned as mere cultists. And, to choose an almost contrary instance, the literary intelligentsia have joined forces with harmless lovers of popular music in combating the self-styled 'serious' concert public, as it were, to create a place in the pantheon for Jacques Offenbach. The ranking of composers and musical genres is, however, made difficult by the fact that, generally speaking, a socially definable carrier stratum participates in several musical genres at once, and conversely each genre involves several carrier strata. In abstract terms this means that it is not individual social and musical strata that must be brought into mutual relation to each other, but rather groups of strata, i.e. large segments of the hierarchy.

2

Historians who have given little thought to the significance of 'dogmatics' in jurisprudence or theology often use this term with deprecation, as though it referred to some forbidden precinct that a scholar dare not enter lest he prostitute himself as a scholar and join the ranks of the prophets (as Wilamowitz accused Nietzsche of doing). However, as Erich Rothacker has suggested, we must distinguish between the *primary* establishment of dogmas or norms, which is emphatically not the business of scholarship, and the *secondary* elaboration and systematisation of the propositions thus received, which is a thoroughly scholarly activity and, though secondary, anything but subordinate. (We would be at a loss to justify the scientific status of jurisprudence if we considered it outside the bounds of scholarship to elucidate the presuppositions, consequences and implications of received propositions.)

We have seen that aesthetic and compositional norms represent premises of musicology by being a condition of possibility for selecting the works that 'belong to history'. Now, these norms are at the same time an object of investigation for the aesthetics or poetics of music. And by 'poetics' we mean dogmatics in the non-pejorative sense of the word, i.e. the systematisation of those ideas and categories, tenets and criteria that, implicitly or explicitly, underlie the musical judgments and decisions of an age, or of one of the 'trends' within that age. It is not nearly enough just to collect the pronouncements on music in general, or on individual works in particular, that have been handed down from a particular age and to piece them together into a history of reception like so many stones in a mosaic. On the contrary, we must also try to reconstruct the assumptions and preconditions that led some works to be admitted into the standard repertory, or at least to be remembered, while others were not. Musical dogmatics, meaning the codification and systematisation of the aesthetic and compositional norms behind a style or trend of a particular age, rests on the foreknowledge that the works in our imaginary museum were selected not as a result of an accumulation of coincidences or arbitrary decrees, but on the basis of judgments and decisions that once formed a coherent pattern – a pattern that contemporaries might not have been conscious of but which nevertheless influenced their behaviour.

Accordingly, the aim of this dogmatics of art would be to discover, amidst the scattered documents, traces of a mode of cognition that formed what linguists would call the 'deep structure' to the judgments and decisions of an age: judgments that were formulated in words, and decisions that were simply made without being explicitly justified. Hence, for instance, a discussion of the origins of musical fame in the nineteenth century might proceed from an hypothesis that found scant support in the aesthetics of the time, with its predilection for philosophical systems: that esoteric and exoteric substantiation must always work in conjunction with one another, and that despite the notion of absolute music, success in music has seldom if ever been an exclusively musical matter but invariably draws upon extramusical currents, which serve as the vehicle of a piece's fame without necessarily leaving the imprint of the *Zeitgeist* on the music itself.

Thus, in the case of Wagner and Liszt no less than Schumann and Brahms, we are left to determine the particular constellation formed of the overt, popular traits of their music and the covert features that make up its artificial nature. Despite a widespread but simplistic view to the contrary, it was not entirely for the over-powering effect they had on the emotions of the listener, and actually in spite of the 'ingenious mechanisms' concealed within them, that Wagner's works became famous. Rather it was because of an inseparable cohesion of emotional appeal and technical mastery – an emotional appeal that would have quickly palled and had no more effect than a storm in a teacup without the artifices behind it, and a technical mastery that would scarcely have compelled the listener's interest had it not been for the purposes that it served so triumphantly. Even listeners who abandoned themselves to Wagner's music without preconceptions were inwardly aware that the *alfresco* sensation they felt ultimately stemmed from a mastery of the art of the miniature, a mastery of the subtlest kind imaginable. And in Brahms's case a basically similar dialectical interplay must be developed, this time between thematic manipulation and lied melody, for the conditions of musical fame in the nineteenth century.

Furthermore, once we accept that the idea of a 'dogmatics of art', meaning a codification and systematisation of aesthetic and compositional styles in a given age, represents a viable scholarly programme, the problem of historical relativism that so unnerves and torments many historians appears in a new light. For within the confines of 'art dogmatics' judgments and selections are not sub-stantiated relative to a single subject – which is to say they are not simply left to the whims and caprices of the individual. Rather, they are intersubjective and 'disputable' in the scholastic sense of the word that lies behind that constantly misconstrued aphorism 'De gustibus non est disputandum'. (Dogmatics in jurisprudence allows us to make decisions by rigorous deduction rather than merely leaving them to a sense of justice.) As the guiding principles behind a system of music aesthetics prove more and more amenable to reconstruction we can, with ever greater confidence, refer to individual judgments or decisions from the past as being in or out of keeping with their respective periods, instead of just taking on trust and meekly registering all utterances whatsoever as being docu-ments on the *Zeitgeist*.

In consequence, an historian who thinks about value-judgments rather than simply making or accepting them need not perpetually brood about historical relativism. Instead, he can see himself as confronted by a problem that can be solved by scholarly means: the problem of determining, for a system of aesthetic norms, both its logical structure and its historical scope, i.e. its limitations in respect of time and locality, social level and ethnic origin. For the moment, though not of course for ever, we can hold in abeyance the twisted dialectics at work between the concepts 'relative' and 'absolute' by posing questions of an historical and empirical nature. Without puzzling over the fact that, taken as a whole, systems of historical norms are in turn 'relative', we can try to understand their internal composition and localise them to particular ages and social levels, thereby marking out an area in which we can move with a freedom and confidence that will not easily be shaken by the problems of relativism, even though ultimately these problems will return to haunt us. This is not to advocate the suppression of metaphysical difficulties in favour of naive empiricism, but to say that we ought not to fall prey too often to the temptations of letting ourselves be distracted by philosophical paradoxes from pertinent and eminently practicable tasks. It is bad scholarly form to mock the things we can accomplish by continually pointing out to those trying to accomplish them that their ultimate goals are unattainable.

Nor is it necessary, for the purposes of reconstructing past systems of aesthetic norms, to swear allegiance to the historicists' tenet that every age has the right to serve as its own measure – a tenet that force of habit has endowed with an aura of unassailability but whose meaning is not absolutely clear. We could, like Ranke, give this proposition a basis in theology (in God's eyes an age is never merely the means to the end of another era but exists in its own right); it also admits of a cynically functionalist interpretation (however barbaric a system of norms may seem to enlightened observers, the question is whether it fulfilled the integrative function for which it was conceived). In either case it is equally unclear whether this historicists' thesis is meant to proscribe 'extrinsic' judgments altogether or solely restrict the historian within his *métier*. Does it claim that the historian's task is to understand unfamiliar systems of norms from the inside and not to judge them from some external vantage point (which is, after all, the entire intent and purpose of the systematisation of styles by dogmatics)? Or does it also condemn 'valuations' that go beyond the reconstruction of 'value-relations' as being by their very nature illegitimate and misconceived, not only for the historian who dutifully keeps within the limits of what he can reach using empirical and analytical

methods, but for anyone and everyone? In daily usage this proposition, to put it crudely, contains one part platitude and another part
ideology; and the insidious thing about it is that the step from the
one to the other almost always passes unnoticed.

3

Tradition critique has always been a major part of the science of
history. Historians do not begin their work from nothing, examining primary sources with no suppositions or preconceptions, but are
occupied in disproving, modifying or corroborating previous historical accounts of events and circumstances from the past. Incorporated into a method, this distrust of surviving records gives rise to
questions without which primary sources would remain mute and
meaningless. It is previous histories that provide the motivation for
writing history; facts do no more than supply the material needed
to follow up this initial impetus.

Now, when we subject the artistic canon, which is a premise of
music historiography, to an historical critique, we are indulging in
tradition critique no less than when we cast doubt on received historical narratives. Yet this tradition critique takes an essentially
different form from the customary procedures of history. Historical critique of the musical canon is indirect: it does not confront
aesthetic norms and criteria directly with arguments from aesthetics, but draws on elements that are found in conjunction with
norms without being norms themselves. However, as mentioned
above, it is precisely when we reflect on the preconditions and consequences of a norm that the possibility exists of rationally discussing our beliefs instead of leaving them to irrational decisionism.

Some works owe their aesthetic prestige, and their standing as
stylistic paradigms within their respective genres, to the ascen-
dancy of an historical myth, and will forfeit their fame the moment
that myth is exploded by historical critique. Taken by itself, Palestrina's *Missa Papae Marcelli* may very well be a work of unimpeachable classical perfection; but the normative status that it received
as the mass that purportedly convinced the reluctant Council of
Trent of the appropriateness of polyphonic church music for the
liturgy will topple, or at least totter, once the surviving anecdotes
about it are unmasked as mere legend.

Other works have an historical impact that only came to light as a
result of historical research, 'impact' being understood to mean an
effect on later works rather than survival in the standard repertory

or in memory. Though not in itself an aesthetic factor, this impact nevertheless constitutes an authority which, alongside artistic merit, helps to establish the canon upon which music historiography is based. The operas of the Florentine Camerata do not belong to history on their own aesthetic merit as works of art, but rather because of their consequences, in marking the 'beginnings of opera'. If it were not for their effect on Monteverdi, particularly in his Venetian rather than the earlier Mantuan years, the Florentine experiment would scarcely have stood out from the general run of antiquarian endeavours ranging from the humanistic ode to Vincentino's chromatic and enharmonic tunings. The claim that a work deserves a commanding place in history simply for having been the first of a genre with a long and important subsequent history is by no means a universally accepted principle. Indeed, it is more likely to prove fallible. Moreover, it is questionable whether the 'beginnings of opera' can be dated at all, as the stylistic, dramaturgical and social features that go to make up this genre coalesced only gradually. Hence it would not be absurd to relegate Florentine opera to the realm of peripheral experiments from which earlier music historians had extracted it on the basis of the supposition that there actually exists a 'birth of opera' which this music represents, along with the contemporaneous deaths of Palestrina and Lasso. The correction of this view would mean that, by a process of historical critique involving a change of historiographical principles and distrust of the notion of 'birth', a work would lose the historical stature formerly attributed to it.

As mentioned above, the conception of novelty as an aesthetic criterion contains an element which, being historical, is subject to historical critique. If the novelty that sustains the prestige of a work proves on closer examination to have been mere simulation, a change will be wrought in the aesthetic quality of the work without a single note of its text having been tampered with. The aesthetic value-judgment will fall victim to an objective historical one, a normative proposition to an empirical one. The stubbornness with which Josef Matthias Hauer persisted in claiming to be the first twelve-note composer was apparently an offshoot of his conviction that the dodecaphonic method was not so much an invention as a discovery, for which, as in the natural sciences, priority is all-important. But it was no less an offshoot of his belief that the 'first-time-ever factor' in history, as Adorno called it, is also part of artistic quality in music, and that a work forfeits its aesthetic authenticity when it is displaced from its chronological position.

But the novelty criterion is open to historical critique in yet another respect. The insights of history can be used to set temporal and social limits to the applicability of this category. The proposition that music must be innovative to be authentic may be unquestionably valid for artificial music from the eighteenth century onwards, but it is dubious when applied to twelfth- or thirteenth-century music, not to mention liturgical plainchant. Up to now, however, it has been the cornerstone of every history of medieval music. The evolution of thirteenth-century music was described by Friedrich Ludwig, who established the basic traits of this period, as a succession of compositional innovations, each emerging from its predecessor, rather than as, say, a series of stages in which old and new existed side by side as integral parts of a liturgical corpus that represented a unified musical system.

One device resorted to by historians in altering the standard musical canon is argument by analogy. If the qualities that have hitherto made a particular work seem outstanding are found to recur in another work, then the status of the one is diminished or that of the other magnified. In any case there will be no avoiding a change in the constitution of our imaginary museum, and, paradoxical though it sounds, the quantity of works associated with a normative standard contributes to its quality.

It is a universally accepted commonplace that written history bears the imprint of the age in which it is written. Yet this does not necessarily mean that the past is distorted or maligned. It can also mean that not all insights into the past are possible at all times. (What Wölfflin had to say about art applies equally to art history.) It is doubtless the case that a given present has special affinities to many past epochs, affinities that reveal the meaning and internal cohesion of their events, affairs and works of art (though, as already mentioned, sympathy is not the only way of arriving at profound historical insights). It is no accident that mannerism happened to be recognised as a style in its own aesthetic right, and not simply as a symptom of the waning of the Renaissance, during the age of expressionism. Nevertheless we should be wary of generalising too hastily the interdependence and affinity that exist between the *Zeitgeist* and the opportunities for historical insight. The fact that in the 1930s, an age infested with political harangues, students of German language and literature felt drawn – for no apparent reason – to the Biedermeier period proves beyond the shadow of a doubt that art history, like art itself, often declines to reflect its surroundings and instead seeks refuge in its antitype.

8

The 'relative autonomy' of music history

The 'relative autonomy' of art and art history is a Marxist category
– but not exclusively so. Friedrich Engels used the term in his
letters of the 1890s in order to protect the Marxist 'base versus
superstructure' schema from charges of philistinism by conceding
primacy to economic considerations only as a 'last resort'. Yet even
within Marxism itself, or among those authors who wish to pass for
Marxists, the precise meaning of the autonomy principle is by no
means clear, and the function that attaches to it changes with the
polemical currents of the age.

Nowadays no-one even remotely familiar with the discussions
of aesthetic autonomy would dispute the proposition that it is not a
principle divorced from and lording over history so much as a
phenomenon that has historical limitations and is subject to historical change. The problem lies in deciding on its historical scope, as
this entails probing the connotations of a term which seems at times
so broad as to encompass what Heinrich Besseler called 'presentation music' (*Darbietungsmusik*), as opposed to 'everyday music'
(*Umgangsmusik*), and yet can be so tightly construed as to collapse
into a mere equivalent of the principle of art for art's sake.
'Presentation music', meaning music that is not a constituent part
of some larger, extramusical process but exists as a source of entertainment in its own right, is a phenomenon that has been with us
since time immemorial, whereas the doctrine of art for art's sake is
a nineteenth-century slogan coined, not by the bourgeoisie, as
Marxist disparagers of this doctrine have claimed, but rather by
bohemians harbouring distinctly anti-bourgeois sentiments even
though safely ensconced in the niches of bourgeois society.

There is another reason why it is so difficult to separate autonomous music from functional music. Certain musical functions
such as entertainment, conviviality, edification or official pomp
hover in some middle region between 'everyday music' and
'presentation music'. They are not simply interpolations in extramusical processes, nor do they have an independent existence and
significance of their own; instead they allow the emphasis to fall
now on autonomy, now on functionality. Even so, some musical
genres of the eighteenth to twentieth centuries were definitely or

primarily autonomous. Hence there are practical historiographical reasons – and since no 'one and only' concept of autonomy exists we cannot very well evade considerations of practicality – for striking out on a terminological middle path between one notion of autonomy so broad as to be equivalent to 'presentation music' and another so confined as to mean art for art's sake. For our purposes a musical creation is autonomous (1) if it manages to raise and enforce a claim to be heard in its own right, thus giving form precedence over function, and (2) if it constitutes a work of art in the modern sense, i.e. a work freely conceived and executed with no influence on the part of a patron or purchaser as regards its content or external form.

Still, aesthetic autonomy is not a firmly datable fact that might be summed up in the claim that, since the eighteenth century, all 'art' deserving of the name has been autonomous. On the contrary, it represents a process whose origins are shrouded in obscurity and whose final outcome is, for the present, still uncertain. Instead of passing categorical judgments as to whether music is or is not autonomous it is more appropriate to describe it in detail so as to show to what extent and in what respects it possesses autonomy.

The polyphonic mass of the fifteenth and sixteenth centuries, being music of ritual, would have been classified by Besseler as 'everyday music'. Yet it was not unthinkable for a composer to stand out as an individual, i.e. to attain that *ostentatio ingenii* ('flaunting of genius') for which Glarean upbraided Josquin des Prez. Nor was the aesthetic principle behind the cyclic unification of the various parts of the ordinary, which are kept separate in liturgical practice, entirely in line with the ritual function of the mass.

Seventeenth- and eighteenth-century court music was part of the ceremonial pomp that served to further the fame of the ruler and the self-image of court society. Yet composers were not only permitted to display individuality both in real life and within their works, they were actually encouraged to do so. Moreover, in the category of 'good taste' that arose in the seventeenth century, aesthetic and social elements merged into one: judgment in art not only existed as a separate entity but also served as a means of social demarcation. (The 'taste' which one did or did not possess was determined not by the individual but by group convention.)

Bourgeois art, according to a thesis advanced by Jürgen Habermas, is meant to 'satisfy those residual needs that are suppressed in daily social intercourse'. The functions of conviviality, edification and ceremonial pomp grew less and less important for a musical public that came to represent a 'lonely crowd'. Mass society does not hinder but actually favours solitary absorption in works of art (convivial culture flourishes only within small circles). Consequently, to take aesthetic contemplation – or its popular but degenerate form, introversion and emotional self-indulgence – as a mode of behaviour befitting an autonomous art would appear to be less a bourgeois phenomenon than a feature that will rear its head wherever loneliness and isolation follow in the wake of mass culture to become the hallmarks of a society, be it bourgeois or not.

Even if we take the writing rather than the reception of music as our starting point it is still virtually impossible to consign the autonomy principle to a single spot within social history, i.e. to construe it as a notion of exclusively bourgeois origin and character. True, autonomous music, being an outgrowth of bourgeois society, is subject to market forces, even when these are mitigated by patronage. Yet it is thoroughly anti-bourgeois in spirit, at times even harking back to feudalism, in its resistance to certain market principles – for example the replication of successful models, which would cause it to forfeit its claims as an art and stoop to the level of trivial music.

Besides being a social fact that we can view in the broad context of the increasing complexity and independence of the various spheres of life, aesthetic autonomy is a factor in the making of aesthetic judgments. Functional music was condemned to a subsidiary status in the nineteenth century; and it is difficult to decide whether it fell into disrepute as a result of a decline in the quality of practical forms of music, or conversely whether it lapsed into triviality by adapting to the prejudices that had already been formed against it.

Equally ambiguous, both in a material and in a socio-psychological sense, is the relation between art and craftsmanship that emerged in the nineteeth century. In a world characterised by the division, alienation and heteronomous dispensation and administration of labour, art took on the appearance of an autonomous activity. It became a model and paradigm for non-alienated labour simply because, in contrast to manufactured goods, it remained attached to the principle of undivided labour that once applied to the production of handmade items (utopias thrive on nostalgia). The dignity of craftsmanship that art upheld was a residuum of pre-industrial bourgeois society in an industrial age which, though beginning as a bourgeois era, came to be bureaucratised into forms shared by bourgeois and non-bourgeois societies alike.

On the other hand, art, being free, exempted itself from the role fulfilled by craftsmanship of serving functions and carrying out commissions. Robert Schumann's distinction between the 'poetic' dimension to music (by which he meant its essence as art) and its 'mechanical' side harbours a contempt of craftsmanship as something a composer must master but never put on display (workmanship should be kept secret). The free art of the bourgeoisie is, in its scope, a direct descendant of the *ars liberalis* of the aristocracy. True, the latter centred on music theory and hence on the contemplation of the tonal system rather than, as in the case of free art, aural phenomena. Yet both the 'freedom' inherent in an *ars liberalis* and the autonomy of nineteenth-century art were taken to mean exemption from the dictates of necessity, from social and economic pressures.

Aesthetic autonomy is also the result of an historical process in yet another sense, in addition to being an 'institution' that evolved over centuries and is still evolving. Besides figuring in the 'aesthetics of production', autonomy is a category within the 'aesthetics of reception': works of music that were not conceived as autonomous creations have, since the nineteenth century, been treated as such, their original mode of existence being transformed into another without significant misrepresentation or disfiguration. Undoubtedly, one of the most decisive events in nineteenth-century music history was the rediscovery, or rather simply the discovery, of Bach's music and the conferring upon it of aesthetic autonomy. Having been abstracted from its set purposes, this music became the paradigm and *locus classicus* of one of the pivotal thoughts behind absolute music: the perfect dovetailing of extreme complexity of structure with intensity of expression. And this reinterpretation was not simply a matter of whim open to later retraction. On the contrary, the 'autonomisation' of early music and the 'historicisation' of the repertory that took place in the mid nineteenth century are simply opposite sides of the same coin. A piece of music retains its currency when deprived of its original historical setting, not merely as a relic and document of a bygone age but as an aesthetic presence of virtually undiminished impact, however much its actual substance may have altered. Art can be preserved or restored without thereby losing its meaning, whereas the political and social fabric of which it was once part is dead beyond recall.

It would thus appear that historiography too is affected by the radical difference between aesthetic and political evidence in their historical essence. The further an age recedes into the past, the more faded becomes our image of its socio-political events and structures, and the more its art works are thrust into the foreground, creating the impression that they had always been the hallmarks of their age. In the course of historical reconstruction, anything that happens to survive the past in the form of an aesthetic presence will automatically receive an emphasis that it did not have at the time of its origin (as is more obviously true of architecture than of music). The worn-out cliché about the true nature of an era only being recognisable in retrospect is merely a perverse way of saying that we consider things that survive the past to be more essential and characteristic than things that perish. However, only a metaphysician will be able to decide whether or not posterity's view of an age is more 'correct' than the age's view of itself, i.e. whether or not cultural and social historians should be given the final say.

By now it should be clear that aesthetic, or 'relative', autonomy is an historical phenomenon whose existence cannot be denied even if its scope and significance are still open to debate. Yet this is not enough to warrant a music historian's using the autonomy principle as the mainstay of his history in the manner of, say, Hugo Riemann, who described the evolution of music as a continuum of formal transformations, or of the Russian formalists, who treated music history as an internal process kept in motion by the fact that the consolidation of a style, and the resultant stereotyping of aesthetic perception, call for a constant renewal of artistic devices. We do not have to deny the existence of aesthetic autonomy as an idea that influenced history from the eighteenth to twentieth centuries in order to maintain that it constitutes, at the very most, an object of historical investigation but never a basic historiographical axiom (though there should be no question about the heuristic advisability of proceeding mainly from the principles of the age under study, in this case adopting the nineteenth-century conception of art, in order to understand the evolution of its music). Thus the consequences of aesthetic autonomy for music history depend less on the fact of its existence than on the way it is interpreted. And the interpretations it has received contrast starkly with each other. In its relation to society, aesthetic autonomy has been variously construed as a moral precept, as an instance of bad faith, and as what Ernst Bloch has called a 'concrete utopia'.

Being subject to market forces, a composer feels himself at the mercy of a social compulsion, whether economic or psychological, or at least a temptation, to maintain a manner that has proved successful and thereby to become, in a manner of speaking, an epigon of himself. (However difficult it may be to determine through tangible facts, we almost always sense the dividing line between a self-imitative 'manner' and a distinctive 'style'.) Financial motives come into conflict with aesthetic ideals that the composer himself considers paramount. (Public reaction is often divided on this point: a desire for novelty is held in check by an opposite desire for repetition, and the formula for success lies in the 'semblance of familiarity' as found, for instance, in the actually quite original melodies of Tchaikovsky.). The autonomy principle reveals its moral side in the axiom that a composer must resist social pressures for the sake of the integrity of his music. And it is this axiom that has made music history since the eighteenth century, economic forces notwithstanding. Objective aesthetic integrity finds its subjective correlate in moral integrity.

In Adorno's writings this same appeal to morality lies behind his thesis that aesthetic autonomy, as upheld by Schoenberg and Webern at the price of social alienation, can mean not merely rejection of, but also, and more importantly, resistance to, historical realities that portend the doom of art. In his view, the internal evolution of music expresses, reflects or issues from developments within society as a whole, regardless of whether the composer is aware of this fact. Whatever happens within a work is an aid to understanding events within history itself. By rigorously pursuing technical problems in composition, entrusting themselves to the 'propensity of the material' and resisting outside influences and demands, composers convey truths about the society they live in more accurately and more tellingly than would be possible by straightforward, unsophisticated description. To express the *status quo*, however, is to distance oneself from it. Art consents to evil by idealising it, not by illustrating it; and to Adorno's way of thinking it was the 'formalism' of the New Music which, far from hindering illustation, made it possible in the first place. Autonomy contains and, as it were, takes full advantage of an insight into reality. And any art that is autonomous rebels against the miseries of existence instead of falling victim to them by conforming.

Now, once the historian has accepted the proposition that music, in its internal evolution, mirrors external developments in society at large precisely by eluding their direct influence and focussing on problems of technique, he must face a consequence in his methodology: that although he presents music history not by itself but in relation to social history, he must nevertheless cling to the autonomy principle in his interpretations even while he goes beyond it in thought. Works of music receive their documentary or historiological significance not in isolation from, but precisely by virtue of, their essence as art. Thus, in the course of that 'social decoding' expounded and practised by Adorno, the element of artifice must never be given short shift even though aesthetic isolation has been broken. It is precisely its autonomy that makes music such an eloquent commentator on society. For the interpreter this means that he must never lose sight of autonomy, even when infringing against it, in his attempts to decipher the message of the music. Were music incapable of using form alone to express what it has to say there would be no point in its expressing it at all.

Marx rigorously maintained that art represents a piece of ideology or bad faith, one of those 'phantasms of the human brain' that distort our view of the material world, and that the aesthetic autonomy in which modern art believes itself to be thriving is a delusion that must be exploded. But this severe ideological critque of art was not his only word on the subject, nor his last one. It was simply the more visible portion of a theory whose reverse side is a utopian conception of art. That the independence of art should prove to be a deception is a feature, not of art *per se*, but of the condition of alienation in which it is made to exist under the law of the division of labour. In a free society art would be truly autonomous, serving no other end than the self-fulfilment of those who practise it. (Two questions, however, are left unanswered, namely whether this utopia of non-alienated labour on all levels of society is not, in large part, improbable and hopelessly abstract, and whether its minimal chances of ever being put into effect are already prefigured in the artist's activities, which would make art a paradigmatic – and potentially realisable – instance of non-alienated labour.)

Marxist aesthetics and art histories of recent decades try to have it both ways. On the one hand, music of the past is presented as a fragment of ideology, conditioned by the structure of the society in which it originated: the 'humanity' implicit in Gluck's or Haydn's music is taken to express the 'bad faith' with which their age glossed over and trivialised the very real inhumanity that governed social practice. But on the other hand, major works are thought to have a substance or 'meaning' that enables them to tower above their own times and be passed down to later ages of a radically different social structure. Accordingly, 'humanity' in music is at one and the same time a deception, blinding us to the miseries of existence and making us tolerate the intolerable, and a prefiguration of a future reign of 'liberty' and 'human fulfilment', in which great music will finally achieve the true social function that it had contained in embryo all along.

Hence, in their day-to-day factional disputes, Marxists either lean towards ideology critique or proceed from the relative autonomy of art – generally turning historiological pathos into penny-dreadful catchphrases in the process. Which side they take depends on their polemical or apologetic ends in view. When they intend to show the functions that music serves in non-socialist society they invoke the base–superstructure schema of ideology critique. When, however, they wish to characterise a social order that approximates to perfect socialism they concede to music a human significance free from all ideological and utopian double meaning, as though the end of 'alienation' that Marx foresaw with the passing of the old order were somehow immediately in the offing.

The concept 'relative autonomy' – the expression of the belief that music goes beyond its deceitful ideological function to propound a partial utopia – is, accordingly, one of the assumptions that underlie the theory (and the politics) of the 'cultural legacy' that socialism will inherit once it comes of age. Yet it is not sufficiently clear whether this assumption, like Marx's much-quoted pronouncement on the afterlife of ancient art, is meant to be a classicist precept or a thesis of reception history. Is the present-day meaning of art works – their message to us and the cause of their being handed down at all – identical to their original meaning? Or does it result from the researches of reception historians, whose task it is not only to discover but to reconstrue?

The 'double truth' at work in the Marxist theory of art, i.e. the distinction between ideology critique and classicism, between the repudiation of art as 'deception' and its salvation as 'prefiguration', is not only implicit in Marx's own writings. It is also the upshot of a contradiction that even non-Marxist art theorists have been at pains to convey ever since historical awareness came into conflict with the metaphysic of beauty around 1800. Namely, should a musical creation be deciphered as documentary evidence for use in social or intellectual histories? Or should it be interpreted as a work of art existing in its own right, its historical implications (whose existence no reasonable structural analyst would deny) being a function of its form rather than, *vice versa*, its form being a function of its documentary aspect? Construed in Marxist terms, the 'autonomisation' of art works – i.e. the process whereby music maintains its message, or makes it discernible for the first time, long after its original environment has perished – might mean that the ideological function once served by a piece of music has given way to aesthetic autonomy as it enters a society freed from the stigma of 'alienation'. In this liberated society, aesthetic autonomy would prove to be 'anthropological' as well, for music would have no other task than to function as a stepping stone to self-fulfilment for those who chose to express or recognise themselves in music.

Orthodox Marxists interpret the relative autonomy of art so as to suppress its utopian aspect, albeit with the purpose of offsetting a misuse of the base–superstructure schema by 'vulgar Marxists'. Granted, orthodox Marxists concede some interplay between base and superstructure rather than positing a unilateral dependency; but they insist that the 'final arbiter' is always and invariably the economic structure. As applied to history, this view implies that the tangled skein of technical, aesthetic, psychological, social and economic factors open to empirical investigation must always be interpreted on the basis of one single, unalterable hierarchy.

The problems involved in tackling the hierarchy thesis are virtually labyrinthine, and a music historian may be excused for shying away from them. However, a few comments (of no scholarly pretensions) cannot be avoided.

First of all, this fixed, unalterable hierarchy of explanatory arguments comes into conflict with methodological 'pluralism' which – rather than some 'idealist' concept – might be said to represent the current alternative to the Marxist theory of history. The polemical barb to pluralism is a criticism aimed at two targets. The first is dogmatism. Dogmatism insists that there is one and only one true relation between historical events, i.e. it onesidedly favours the element of 'mirror reflection' rather than 'construct' in its view of the relation of the *historia rerum gestarum* to *res gestae*. The other target is decisionism, the result of an extreme sceptical standpoint. Decisionists take the existence of competing interpretative schemes – i.e. the fact that an historical process (such as the emergence of atonality from 1907) can be explained, not only in terms of the history of compositional technique, but also in terms of social history or by analogy to breaks with tradition in literature and painting – to show that there is virtually no limit to the number of historical connections producible by historians, and that facts will accommodate themselves with surprisingly little resistance to the most disparate models brought to bear upon them.

In consequence, the crucial problem for methodological pluralism, if it is to avoid scepticism, lies in developing criteria for making and justifying conclusions as to how 'deep' explanatory models go and how well they are supported by facts. Trivial as it may seem to demand that historiographical theses pass empirical muster, this demand can only be partially fulfilled at best, since it is not clear just which facts make up the yardstick against which the validity of a model is to be measured. At times it is even the choice of model that determines which facts are relevant and which are not.

Events can be traced to a multitude of causes, with intentionality and causality, intellectual history, social history and the history of compositional technique all existing side by side or competing with each other. As a result, the explicative historian finds himself in the same boat as his counterpart, the narrative historian, who must deal with a teeming mass of processes. Both are faced with the task of selecting and highlighting on a rational basis. The distinctions between motivations and conditions, between causes and underlying forces, with which histories normally function, are vague and theoretically unfounded, but they are unavoidable unless we are willing to concede equal weight to every cause discoverable for a given event and to let the selection and gradation of individual instances depend solely on the historian's cognitive interests. It is perfectly obvious – or, in the case of non-Marxists, ought to be perfectly obvious – that an historian has the right, as a scholar, to pose the questions that happen to interest him, and that the relation between causes and ancillary conditions will alter according to the questions posed (a cause in the history of the symphony can be a condition in a biography of Beethoven, and *vice versa*). Yet this consideration need not hamper us in distinguishing between central and peripheral questions. This is not to say that some explanations are more 'correct' than others, or that they are – to use an often mindlessly applied phrase – 'closer to the truth'. But they may well be of greater moment or more basic.

This plurality of explanations, all on an equal footing with each other, is not an ultimate conclusion reached by the historian so much as an heuristic principle that he proceeds from in order to keep his options open. Once he resolves to present the results of his investigations as clearly and as convincingly as possible he finds himself compelled to select and gradate the causes that he has drawn upon. And obviously he should spare no efforts to give his decisions a rational foundation instead of merely invoking, in the decisionist manner, his right to make an arbitrary selection in the face of an otherwise impenetrable chaos of open possibilities.

Now, it poses no serious threat to the notion of a hierarchy of historical causes if we admit that it is thoroughly legitimate, and in some scholarly situations even advisable, for the historian to ask questions which are less basic or momentous than others. But even so, he should beware of equating a _logical_ gradation of explanatory arguments (i.e. the hierarchy ultimately attained after his initial state of heuristic indecision) with an _ontological_ gradation. To maintain that the 'deep' causes of an event in music history are to be found in biological or even biochemical and ultimately physical processes is obviously as indisputable on ontological grounds as it is nonsensical in terms of the logic of science. Yet it is by no means certain just how far 'down' our deliberations can go without losing their meaning and relevance and straying into the realm of the absurd. For the moment, there is no end in sight to the controversy as to whether music-historical facts should be traced to sociological, or even to psychological and anthropological explanations. Nevertheless, it should be plain which dangers the historian must try to avoid: decisionism – the arbitrary gradation of historical explanations by individuals or factions as occasion demands; dogmatism – a preconceived bias toward a fixed and unalterable hierarchy of historical causes; and irrelevance – the recourse to causes which, though real, lack a proper bearing on the subject under investigation. (Generally speaking, no-one who wishes to understand an event in music history will seek enlightenment in physiological analysis, even if he does have occasion to refer to Beethoven's deafness.)

As an alternative to the Marxist theory of history, the pluralism thesis means that the historian will refuse to presuppose the existence of a fixed gradation of explanatory arguments even though his ultimate goal is to arrange them into a hierarchy. Instead, he prefers to strike out on the thornier heuristic path of assuming and trying out a variety of equally acceptable causal hypotheses at first, in the belief that the further progress of human knowledge lies precisely in the dialectics at work between the pluralist open-mindedness and indecision with which he sets out and the systematic unity and fixity that he wishes to achieve, not for history in general but within the confines of his own specific topic.

A second reason for distrusting the Marxist theory of history, besides the general one of not wanting to close the options that pluralism has opened for us, is logical in nature. While non-Marxists do not find the base–superstructure schema *a priori* objectionable, they regard it as worthy of consideration at the most as a hypothetical construct in need of empirical verification, not as an irrefragable axiom. True, the verification method cannot be wielded in an historical discipline with the same authority as in the natural sciences; as already mentioned, there is seldom a shortage of historical facts to be cited in support of different or even contradictory interpretative schemes. Nevertheless, so long as the scientific community keeps a safe distance from the various groupings of dilletants and zealots, there is no reason why historians should yield to an irrational decisionism born of extreme scepticism. The fact that they incline by nature to adopt a controversial or sceptical stance when discussing principles does not mean that, faced with a concrete instance, they are reluctant or unable to agree on the difference between sound hypotheses and rambling speculation. In the day-to-day business of their trade it is less difficult for historians to reach a consensus as to whether a claim is plausible or misguided, soundly argued or riddled with flaws, than one would imagine, considering the vehemence with which they dispute points of principle when advancing theories.

Thirdly, non-Marxists cannot muster much conviction in the idea that economic factors should have been the final arbiter in each and every age of history; indeed they rather tend to reject it. What might have been true of the nineteenth century need not apply to the Middle Ages. In any event, an open and variable system with changing affiliations and emphases among the individual factors is a more plausible model for historians who prefer not to make obeisances to historiological preconceptions. And, if we may be permitted to turn Marx against himself and criticise his own ideology, it seems likely that he has elevated a hallmark of his own age into a general historiographical principle, leaping from empiricism to the philosophy of history in one bound. The Marxist who insists on the primacy of economic considerations 'in the final analysis' is no different from the idealist who views events in history as nothing more than the visible side of changes in consciousness: both reveal a lack of historical acuity by overlooking the fact that the manner in which musical phenomena are historically conditioned is itself conditioned by history, and the structure of the factors that occasion historical change is likewise subject to change. A more enlightening model for historians who have managed to ward off the urge to seek solace in historiological formulae is that variability in substantiation and affiliation which Jacob Burckhardt, in his *Weltge-schichtliche Betrachtungen*, posited among his 'three potencies' of religion, culture, and the state.

Fourthly, even when dealing with an epoch in which economic considerations actually did function as the final arbiter in a system of mutual influences, correlations and dependencies, we might well ask whether, and if so to what extent, art history stands to gain at all by having recourse to economics. 'And ultimately', writes Burckhardt, 'it is not necessary to discover material motives behind the birth of each and every mental and spiritual phenomenon, even if such motives were, in the end, to be found. Once the mind has become self-aware it will continue on its own in the further creation of its world' (*ibid.* p. 60). This self-reflection and self-awareness on the part of the mind points to a relative autonomy in its development that makes all recourse to material bases, though still possible, hardly worthwhile. Even if we concede the primacy of economics in Antiquity we can still doubt the claim that, as theory results from contemplation, contemplation from leisure, and leisure from economic suppression, the music theory of the Ancients cannot be fully comprehended without an analysis of the economic structure of the 'slaveowner society'. We do not have to deny the fundamental significance of economics to be of the opinion that a study of economic conditions will shed little light on the contents or validity of a theory of art. Nor is the belief that the essence of all things will be revealed by probing as deeply as possible into their origins anything more than a typical late-nineteenth-century prejudice once shared by Marx and Nietzsche but now bereft of that ring of the self-evident it once enjoyed. (The search for origins has acquired a bad reputation as 'reductionism'.) Burrowing for roots, rather than taking a mature phase as a point of departure, was a compulsion with which the positivists of the late nineteenth century hoped to offset the classicism of the earlier years of the century. And to choose a reductionist theory other than Marxism as an example, is it really necessary for an understanding of Beethoven's late works to be psychoanalytically enlightened as to his precarious relationship with his nephew Karl? Surely even if the analysis were sound it would have something of the absurdity of the man who tried to explain the causes of the death of Archduke Ferdinand at Sarajevo with a medical disquisition.

Fifthly, it is by no means an established fact that those social factors which are most clearly at work in music history necessarily rank among what social historians would regard as the essential features of the age. Max Weber argued that to distinguish between classes solely on the basis of property, as Marx did to underpin his model of history, is to overlook other types of class structure which scholarship can devise and test against historical fact, and that society can also be partitioned into classes on the basis of 'achievement' or 'status'. Marxists have objected strongly to this thesis, claiming that the opposition of property classes has always been the sole decisive conflict and the motivating principle behind history, while features such as status merely represent 'superstructural' phenomena. (Naturally these same Marxists are careful not to forget the ideological reproach that Weber's elaboration of the notion of class is a philosophical manoeuvre contrived by an endangered bourgeoisie to delude itself and others as to the real, mortal conflict it faces.) However, without entering into sociological disputes, it is obvious to a music historian that the distinction between 'status' classes which Marxists deem secondary has been remarkably influential in the history of art, more so in fact than the conflict of property classes. The notion of the 'educated man', for instance, a figure who was to a large extent the mainstay of nineteenth-century culture, represents a status or social level whose distinguishing features – e.g. a university degree in the case of civil servants, or a base in an office rather than behind a counter in the case of merchants – cannot easily be accounted for in economic terms. In any event, as Burckhardt realised, the historian need not feel intimidated by the claims of economics to be a 'final arbiter', for despite what this metaphor suggests in law, in history the final arbiter is not always the decisive one.

Anyone who singles out the autonomous side of 'relative autonomy' for special emphasis and underplays its relative dependency, without actually denying or ignoring it, will have to put up with charges from Marxist quarters that he is overlooking the key connections which determine music's essence as an historical phenomenon in the first place. Marxist theory turns on a premise that we might call the 'totality postulate': that a history of music (or of any other superstructural phenomenon) written in isolation from history in general is meaninglessly abstract. According to Marx, music is part of ideology and therefore does not have a history of its own; only society as a whole has history. Hence, if music is to be understood in historical terms rather than simply received ideologically, it must be presented against a backdrop predetermined by the current state of productive forces and relations. It follows that what music historians write can claim to be a *history* of music only to the extent that it is not limited to the history of *music*.

This thesis is a challenge and must be met, all the more so as even though non-Marxist musicology[1] has no shortage of research results and historical interpretations of individual works, processes and connections to show for itself, it still lacks a comprehensive view of music historiography that would be something more than a mere encyclopaedic patchwork quilt pieced together from bits of biography, intellectual history, and the history of genres and institutions. Music history is in danger of betraying what its name implies. The notion of intellectual history – i.e. the thought that music history can be told in terms of changes in our ways of thinking, changes that manifest themselves primarily and most clearly in the development of philosophy and religion – has simply collapsed of old age, without even the rhetorical bother of a controversy to hasten its demise. The Russian formalist theory of history was not acknowledged by music historians at the time, and it is now too late to revive it, as certain of its premises have toppled. Finally, methodological pluralism – i.e. the principle of doing without principles, or the idea of dispensing with a fixed hierarchy of bases for historical explanation and instead setting out from an indefinite number of open options and ultimately gradating and linking them so as to characterise the age in question – has up to now produced only a few meagre and sparse attempts at history. However, since at the moment there is scant hope that non-Marxists will reach a consensus on the guiding principles of music historiography,[2] i.e. since uncertainty prevails at present, grappling with Marxist theorems seems all the more urgent, whether the intention is to take from them what is tenable, to reach a higher level of reflection in our own convictions, or simply to clarify matters by dismissing premises that do not apply.

According to the 'totality postulate' music history by itself, far from being autonomous, as its practitioners imagine, is in fact not

---

[1] It is utterly wrongheaded to follow the lead of Marxist polemicists and blanket all non-Marxist musicology under the heading 'idealist', as though opposition to Marx had not budged from its position of a century ago.

[2] Of course, in a lively discipline such a consensus ought not to be taken too far in any case, but at present it is far too weak, a result less of contention than of apathy.

history at all but merely a scrap torn from history with no 'law of motion' of its own. Now, this proposition can be criticised from several standpoints – historiological, epistomological or heuristic. And it will probably suffice here to sketch some of the less demanding practical considerations rather than the far-reaching theoretical ones.

First of all, the principle that historians must 'totalise', as Jean-Paul Sartre put it, suffers from the shortcoming that, however tantalising it sounds in the heat of historiological speculation, it is probably unrealisable in historiographical practice. This is not to accuse the totality principle of being as absurd as its detractors have made it out to be in their caricatures. The idea of history as something whole and integral against which the historian must understand his particular concerns is not directed towards completeness in a quantitative sense: everyone knows this is unattainable. What it does mean is that the image of an overall context – a 'context of contexts' – arises automatically and naturally from the everyday business of writing history, i.e. from the making of connections (it is a trivial misconception that the main task of the historian lies in gathering facts). Hence it would seem that 'History', in that singular form which, while trivial today, is actually a paradox that was not discovered or construed as such until the eighteenth century, is not a conceivable subject for 'history' as an empirical discipline. The existence of an integral, holistic 'History' which is more than a bundle of individual 'histories' is at best an historiological hypothesis; but it can never be grounded in fact, or at least never to our satisfaction. Consequently, distracting and seductive as it is, the totality postulate is impracticable as an ideal for any kind of history that wants to make do with a minimum of speculation. Nor is the notion of an 'exemplary', that is to say 'particular', totality anything more than a contradiction in terms, without even the mitigating virtue of being part of a dialectical process that mirrors the dialectics in the matter itself. To be sure, it makes a tempting postulate to think that an historian with an overall context in view might be able to reveal it in outline when describing a few lesser sub-contexts. But in the daily business of history 'exemplary' analyses turn out to be a few crude formulae applied again and again *ad infinitum* and held to embody the laws of motion in history. (It is characteristic of Marxist history as a whole that it frequently reaches a stature in its theory – and in its critique of non-Marxist history – that far exceeds its actual attainments in historiography.)

Secondly, the decision as to whether social history is part of music history or *vice versa* is not necessarily a choice between mutually exclusive principles, a choice whose rightness or wrongness each and every historian must work out for himself in consultation with the scientific community. Rather, this choice is equally dependent on the historian's particular interests, which can change without thereby becoming illegitimate. For music is at once a work of art and a document. Either it forms the object which the historian wishes to comprehend and around which he marshals his explanations, or it can be simply the material he uses to illustrate structures and processes from social history. No-one questions the scholarly legitimacy of social or cultural histories which find room for music in their panoramas. What does seem puzzling is the claim that these represent the 'real' history of music. In any event, the thesis that a collection of music-historical facts does not make a *history* of music until put in the context of social history is faced with the antithesis that in such a context it ceases to be a history of *music*.

Thirdly, the totality postulate would seem to be an extreme version of a basic rule of hermeneutics, namely that we must pay attention to context if we want to understand a text as it was intended. Now, to a Marxist, 'context' invariably means society as a whole. Yet the actual hermeneutic problem that has dogged the context rule from the outset lies in finding a rational basis for deciding, in each particular case, just where to set the limits of its context so as to allow for a satisfactory understanding, satisfactory in respect both of the object to be interpreted and of the end the interpretation is meant to serve. Not only can a context be too narrow, it can also be too broad. To choose a concrete example, if we wish to avoid misunderstanding some of the concepts and phraseology of Eduard Hanslick's *The Beautiful in Music* it is useful to know that the early chapters were published separately before the later ones had even been written, and hence that many of its points should be read in the context, not of the book as a whole, but of their respective chapters. Similarly, there is little point in bringing society into an account of the relations between sonata form, tonality and chromaticism in the nineteenth century. It is sheer dogmatism born of overly strict adherence to the party line to brand internal approaches of this sort as 'unhistorical', as though the history of composition could not be written in an intelligible and coherent form, or would be worthless even if it could. Admittedly it is no easy matter to devise criteria for deciding when a context is the right size for its subject: the delimitation of context, no less than the pre-knowledge that any interpreter draws upon, indeed must draw upon, is subject to the dialectics of the hermeneutic circle. Deciding how much latitude to give an interpretation has to be governed in each instance by a sense of proportion – a sense which has always been stressed in the humanistic tradition of historiography and does not lend itself to replacement by a dogma prescribing one unchanging context for all occasions, namely society in its entirety.

Fourthly, the materialist totality postulate and its opposite idealist form have a dubious assumption in common: the notion that all contemporaneous things or events possess a unity of substance, or at least a common *Zeitgeist*, against which the non-contemporaneous can be measured. To put this in negative terms, a sense of the basic and profound non-contemporaneity of things that happen to be chronologically simultaneous is still under-developed in Marxist historiography, or has been suppressed by its methodological axioms. True, Marxists have always acknowledged, and have even stressed, the fact that the 'upheaval is slower in the superstructure than in the base'. But they have never been in doubt as to what is 'contemporaneous' or 'in tune with the times' – the base – and what is 'non-contemporaneous' or 'behind the times' – parts of the superstructure. In other words, it is always economics that sets the clock of history. The idea that the history of society as a whole is made up of the sub-histories of its component parts, each 'non-contemporaneous' with the others and none capable by itself of representing the *Zeitgeist*, is foreign to Marxism. (In the 1840s *Zeitgeist* was a typical catchword mainly expressing the notion that a common substance pervades any moment in history; and Marxists have clung to this aspect of the *Zeitgeist* however much they object to its interpretation as an actual 'spirit'.) Yet this *Zeitgeist* against which the historical and historiological status of sub-systems is meant to be measured is a mere fiction, an arbitrary convention – assuming the term is taken seriously in its philosophical sense and not merely used, as journalists legitimately use it, to refer to vague moods that prevail in an age. The most cursory reflection from the standpoint of music history will suffice to expose the belief in a common substance uniting moments of history to burdens it simply cannot bear. Consider, for instance, the fact that music in the late nineteenth century was, in large part, a superior form of romanticism (inferior forms existed as well in literature and painting) in the midst of an age with a positivist philosophy and *Weltanschauung*. This fact is all but irreconcilable with the idea of a uniform *Zeitgeist*, or of a chronological common substance (the economic base is simply the *Zeitgeist* set the right way up by the Marxists). Nor do we have any right to accuse music of 'lagging behind' philosophy. If, for example, we look at the nineteenth century's legacy to our own we might refrain from calling philosophy 'contemporaneous' and music 'non-contemporaneous' and instead come to the exactly opposite conclusion that the 'real' substance of the age came to light not in positivist philosophy but in the music of romanticism. But be that as it may, the point is to describe and elucidate the manner in which positivism and romanticism, for all their 'non-contemporaneity', combined in a way that is fully characteristic of the late nineteenth century. 'Music is different' is a positivist slogan.

Fifthly, it is a blatant misconception to regard the 'history in its entirety' which Marxists try to probe with their totality postulate as being, by analogy with its component sub-histories, a sequence of events that lends itself to narration in principle even if the sheer bulk of material makes narration impossible in practice. Rather, it represents what in Kantian terms is called a 'regulative idea': 'History' in the singular refers to a 'transcendental horizon' within which the tales of sub-systems become histories. However, being a condition that necessarily precedes historical knowledge, this 'transcendental horizon' cannot itself be made an object of historical inquiry. Just like 'nature in its entirety' in the natural sciences, 'history in its entirety' is a conceptual premise in the humanities, and not an empirical object of investigation. It is the ground under the historian's feet, not a thing that he can pick up and scrutinise. When he does talk about it – and he is at perfect liberty to do so – he ceases to be an historian and becomes a philosopher.

Strictly speaking, no-one, not even Hugo Riemann, has actually produced the sort of autonomous music history that Marxists feel called upon to rail against. As mentioned above, the principles of the Russian formalists, whose 'endeavour' it was 'to evolve a self-sufficient science of literature on the basis of properties rooted in the literary material itself',[3] never found favour in musicology. At present, music history parades as a mixture of biography, cultural history, stylistic history and the history of genres and institutions, with stresses varying according to the historian writing or the age depicted. Yet no-one seems disturbed by the fact that these

---

[3] Eichenbaum, *Aufsätze zur Theorie und Geschichte der Literatur*, p. 9.

different approaches sometimes draw on divergent models of history. For instance, the organism model used in histories of genres is out of step with the concept of *Zeitgeist* used in intellectual histories. If musical genres do disintegrate with advanced age it is unlikely that a *Zeitgeist* will always appear at precisely the right moment to seize power and turn its back on exactly those things which, as the organism analogy tells us, are hastening to their demise. Historians are almost always eclectic, and it would be wrong to reproach them for being so: eclecticism may be a somewhat unseemly philosophy, but it is a thoroughly reasonable and practicable one for an historian. Still, to keep our account of the autonomy principle from stagnating into a 'critique of critique' in the form an attack on Marxist objections, it may be useful to give at least a rough sketch of what a history of music based on the rigorous ideas of formalism might look like.

In the original, radical version of formalism advanced by Victor Shklovsky around 1920, the history of an art form was held to consist in the gradual stereotyping of aesthetic perception and the increasing alienation this occasioned as artistic devices were renewed. In other words, new forms are generated, roughly speaking, by the aesthetic attrition of older ones. This approach marks a new departure within intellectual history by breaking with the distinction traditionally made between genesis and validity, between what a work is or means and the conditions under which it came into being. In the latter part of the nineteenth-century, following the collapse of Hegelianism, the 'being' of a work was regularly consigned to aesthetics and its 'becoming' to history. In musicology this view was represented by Philipp Spitta among others. Formalism opposes this partitioning of authority between aesthetics and history. Its main methodological point is to construe the aesthetic aspect of art works not in terms of metaphysics, i.e. using the categories of the philosophy of beauty, but in terms of history. For this alienation of perception caused by the renewal of artistic devices – this estrangement from the familiar and habitual that compels us to alter our aesthetic behaviour and observe art more carefully – is not only a psychological category but, without question, an historical one as well. In formalist theory the history of art takes the form of a chain of innovations. It bridges the gap between 'being' and 'becoming', between a metaphysical aesthetic that takes art works to be art and nothing more, and a type of history that pursues matters of biography, social history and the history of genres without claiming thereby to have penetrated to the inmost essence of art. In the methodology it proposes, formalism offers a version of art *history* that can truly lay claim to being a history of *art*. 'New forms', wrote Shklovsky, 'appear not for the purpose of expressing new content, but to replace old forms which have outlived their artistic viability.'[4]

It is pointless to accuse formalism of being onesided, for it emphasises this onesidedness itself. Formalism makes no attempt to cover all the implications, preconditions and repercussions of art. As in Hanslick's aesthetics of music, its only topic is the specific element of artifice, that which separates art from non-art and one form of art from another. Opponents of formalism who do not wish to become mired in its incidental features should question its vulnerable main thesis that the essential aspect of art is artifice.

Formalists do not claim that the history they tell is the whole of history or the only part worth telling. They merely maintain that an intrinsic history of art as art rather than as documentary evidence for processes in social or intellectual history is, in fact, possible, not as a piecemeal juxtaposition of musical analyses relying solely on chronological order to create the illusion of history, but as a continuous succession of events produced by the dialectics of stereotyping and innovation. Accordingly, restricted as it is, the history of artistic devices is said to have the twin virtues of being of fundamental relevance and of being continuous and self-contained, rather than disjointed and dependent on external conditions. And anyone who looks upon formalism with distrust or enmity will have to challenge the first of these claims on the grounds of ideology critique and disprove the second empirically.

This much said, it is not hard to subject formalism to an incisive critique. In the course of a dispute that has continued for decades several flaws have become clear. First of all, to exclude the possibility that new forms can be generated by new expressive content is a rigorism which, even if intended as a methodological principle and not as an historical observation, is scarcely justifiable. Secondly, innovation does not constitute sufficient grounds for establishing the artistic essence of musical works, i.e. that which distinguishes art from non-art. Thirdly, having a close affinity to modern art, the formalist method is limited in historical scope (to put it bluntly, formalism is a theory of futurism, just as the history of ideas approach it so railed against was a theory of symbolism).

---

[4] Quoted in Eichenbaum, *ibid.* p. 27.

Fourthly, we can escape the stereotyping of aesthetic perception not only by looking forward to the future but by turning to the past, i.e. by electing to restore past art in lieu of innovation. Finally, categories such as 'stereotyping' and 'alienation' have socio-psychological implications, the study of which would inevitably lead us away from an intrinsic history of art as art. (It might turn out that the assumptions drawn upon by formalism from the psychology of perception are valid in some periods for a broad public while in others they apply merely to the artists actively involved in the process of furthering the devices of art, and to a small coterie of initiates.)

However, the real problem lies not in disclosing the weaknesses of formalism but in removing them without sacrificing its pivotal methodological idea: how to write an art *history* that is a history of *art*.

9

Thoughts on structural history

'Structural history' is a fashionable term. For several decades now historians have tended to depict or analyse historical structures, or 'circumstances' as they were called in the nineteenth century, instead of recounting events or sequences of events. The reasons for this are – as Thomas Kuhn maintained of practically all changes of 'scientific paradigm' – partly non-scientific in nature; indeed, the word 'fashionable' would not apply otherwise. To begin with, many historians have let themselves be browbeaten by the prestige of the exact, 'nomothetic' disciplines into adopting an analytical and discursive style to replace, or at least to augment, the epic style of traditional history, where readers were meant to sense the nearness of actual events. (Without necessarily being aware of it, these anti-traditionalist historians address readers who are more likely to project themselves into an historical situation that was endured collectively than to identify with individual heroes towering above the mass of their contemporaries.) Furthermore, the 'administrated world', as Adorno loathingly called modern society, has experienced the intrusion of feelings of anonymity, of depersonalis-

ation and conformism, which cast doubt on the viability that historicists once saw in individuality as a basic category of history. At all
events, these feelings are sufficient cause for historians to root out
half-hidden functional connections in earlier centuries as well and
to put greater stress on them than on individual events and deeds.
At the hands of extreme structuralists, tangible occurrences fade
into mere epiphenomena of structures that must be unearthed and,
as it were, reconstituted before we can begin to sense and argue
their existence.

As early as 1942 Johan Huizinga spoke of a 'metamorphosis of
form within history' since the Industrial Revolution, by which he
meant the *res gestae* rather than the *historia rerum gestarum*. Yet it
is only in most recent times – in the so-called 'fourth age of history'
after Antiquity, the medieval and the modern periods – that 'structures' have received priority over events as constituting the hallmark of the age; and any historian aware of the reflective character
of his discipline, i.e. of the fact that he can use history itself to study
the dependency of an historiographical concept upon his own age,
will feel a need to exercise restraint in applying the principle or
model of structural history to earlier, pre-industrial ages. This,
however, is not to discount the possibility that the industrial age
has provoked a methodological discovery which, having been
made, will now prove to be universal in scope. What applies to
history in general, namely that no historian can afford to take
history as it was before the advent of historical awareness, may also
apply to structural history in particular. Accordingly, structural
history would become a product of the industrial age, not as a fact,
but as a mode of cognition.

Still, it is a plain and simple truth that in the turmoil of the
present, i.e. in history as actually experienced, it is the spectacular
events and deeds that command our attention while the structures
and functional connections that form the underlying 'patterns' to
these tangible events become evident only much later, in retrospect. Hence the outlines of structural history, which have been
clearer since the Industrial Revolution than ever before, are
blurred by the current events that surround us in our daily existence. This re-emergence of events as opposed to structures is perhaps not simply an incidental impression on the part of contemporary observers due to their lack of detachment. Indeed, one might
argue, it shows that precisely in recent times (partly in answer to
the aforementioned tendency to call anonymous and latent systems
the 'makers of history' rather than visible persons or groups) the

course of history has been marked by upheavals so great that a narrative approach stands a better chance of doing justice to them than would an analytic and discursive one. (This, however, is not to plead for a return to the world-hero brand of history.) The methods of structural history, having been devised to deal with the component parts and internal cohesion of systems, are obviously ill-suited to depicting and explaining their collapse or disintegration.

Now, the principle behind the term 'structural history' is not as new as its name, which capitalises on the attraction of the concept of 'structure', would suggest. It simply means that the actions of individuals or groups are always conditioned by an overriding frame of reference which, being of such fundamental importance, properly represents the object of historical inquiry. In this sense, music history has always contained a certain amount of structural history, either in the depicting of institutions and social roles, or in the determining of stylistic or compositional norms and prevailing aesthetic ideas.

This is not to deny that, by and large, music histories were once conceived primarily in terms of composers, forms, genres and even nations (one of the cornerstones of music history is the notion that nations are in mutual conflict for hegemony in music). Music historians drew on three patently incongruous axioms as though they were self-evident truths: (1) that outstanding composers 'make' music history (histories of eighteenth- and nineteenth-century music in particular turned into stylised heroiades); (2) that musical genres evolve in the same way as natural organisms (as though music history were part of natural history); and (3) that this evolution in the musical culture of a nation expresses and embodies its 'national spirit' (as though north and south Germany shared a common 'national' music history).

Now, just as the 'history of events' approach has affinities to political history, so the structural method finds its natural field of application in cultural history. Hence it is understandable that many nineteenth-century music historians such as August Wilhelm Ambros, Wilhelm Heinrich Riehl and Adolf Bernhard Marx should have sought to make past or current musical affairs intelligible by depicting circumstances rather than by reconstructing sequences of events. Once we agree, as would virtually any outside observer well versed in the theory of history, that music history, being part of cultural history, invites or even cries out for a structural approach of some sort, regardless of what name we give it, then it only seems all the more astonishing that the 'history of events' method should have been so influential. Seen in the context of the history of ideas or ideology, this influence has its origins in the precedence given to political history over social history. In music-historical writings this influence is apparent, firstly, in the significance attached to chronological frameworks cobbled together from dates of composition (as though the historical significance of a work depended solely on the moment that it was created rather than on its lifespan within a musical culture). It also appears in the fondness for compiling music histories from the biographies of composers and treating decisive music events, by analogy with political events, as the exploits of heroes. Thirdly its presence can be noted in the aforementioned notion that countries take turns as the dominant 'musical nation' in Europe. And lastly it appears in the premise that music history consists primarily of technical innovations in composition which can, by analogy with political occurrences, be presented as an interlocking chain of events. This premise is doubly suspect, not only because the assumption that works were written 'in reaction' to earlier works must be confirmed in each specific instance rather than simply presupposed wholesale as a hidden implication of the 'history of events' approach, but also because this reduction of past music to a sequence of new ideas (in itself a curious *mésalliance* of the originality aesthetic of the classical and romantic periods and an unconscious emulation of political history) foreshortens the reality of history so drastically that the preparations called for by this method come close to a misrepresentation of fact.

Indirectly, the history of events – which in general (i.e., primarily, political) history stands opposed to the structural approach – has been of enormous significance, as a model whose influence has largely passed unrecognised, for the writing of music history. Its direct influence however has been slight. The motley of biographies, histories of musical genres and national histories that poses as music history is, quite simply, not a history of events, however much it may resemble this approach in point of methodology. In the aesthetics that arose simultaneously and in interaction with music historiography from the eighteenth century onwards, music was viewed, in the Aristotelian sense, as *poiesis* not *praxis*, i.e. as the creation of forms rather than as actions within a social environment. Consequently, the fundamental category is not the 'event' but the 'work'. The categorical distinction between the two can be sketched roughly as follows. Events result from the interplay of actions based on various, and at times conflicting, motives, imagined goals and assessments of a given situation. Their significance lies less in themselves than in their consequences (there is no such thing as a political 'event' without consequences). A work, on the other hand, represents – at least as an 'ideal type' – the concrete realisation of an idea in the mind of an individual; ideally, and in contrast to political history, an intention is realised rather than thwarted. Furthermore, the meaning of a work resides in its aesthetic essence, not in its historical repercussions.

This however is not to say that musical events do not exist. We are perfectly justified in referring to a performance, in which a score, a style of interpretation, certain institutional prerequisites, the expectations of the audience and a sociopolitical situation all coincide, as an event, i.e. a point at which actions and structures intersect. Yet no-one has ever so much as tried to write music history as a history of events, even though music historians almost invariably describe individual events and, in a few instances, actually analyse them. On the contrary, texts as abstracted from acoustical realisations and social surroundings, the institutions that serve as vehicles of musical events, and the categories of music reception – it is these, and not events, which go to make up the corpus of facts that music historians draw upon and in which they try to discern 'patterns' that will enable them to fashion a coherent presentation. Of course one can hold theoretically that it is events, meaning acoustical occurrences taking place within social contexts, that constitute the reality of music, and not works as boiled down into texts. But at present it is hard to envisage just how, in practical terms, music history might possibly be conceived as a history of events.

Nevertheless, it could happen that, by putting the accent on structural history rather than following the model of histories of political events and stressing biography or national history, we would actually further rather than hinder the cause of a history of musical events. Even in social and political history the structural and the 'history of events' approaches are by no means mutually exclusive. On the contrary, they complement one another, notwithstanding a residue of incompatibility that we will never be able to eradicate. For events are sustained by structures, and structures in turn are realised and made manifest in events. The fact that musical events such as the premières in 1868 of *Die Meistersinger* and the German Requiem became historical at all, rather than passing unnoticed, presupposes the existence of certain configurations of social and aesthetic conditions which can be explained as a nexus of functions rather than merely described as accumulations of facts. If, for instance, a musical event such as the first perform- ance of *Robert le diable* can radically change audiences' ideas of the nature of opera, the conditions for this change, i.e. the structures upon which this event impinged, must have been pre-existent; and it is the historian's job, to put it paradoxically, to search for the causes that led an event to become itself a decisive cause.

In this light we can either proceed from events to root out the structures behind them or we can bring a number of structures into relation so as to illuminate a particular event; which path we choose depends on our interest in view. Or, to put it more precisely, anyone who wants to explain an event instead of merely recounting it and hazarding guesses as to the motivation behind it must reconstruct the structures of which it once formed a part; and conversely anyone who wants to make intelligible the changes within a structure, rather than merely displaying the structure in its operative state, must look for the events which, whether from within or without, wrought those changes. In practical terms, this means that to discover new things in one's own field it is almost advisable to turn to complementary fields. As Ernst Bloch put it, anyone who wants to learn about matter should read the idealist philosophers, in whose systems matter was a problem and not a premise.

Still, to say that structural history and the history events are, or ought to be, related is not to say that they merge imperceptibly into one another. The elements of chance and whim (chance in the coincidence of incompatible actions and whim in individual de- cisions) can never be entirely eliminated, not even in the most detailed and subtle presentation of a nexus of functions.

Nevertheless, as hinted above, it proves to be the case that musical events such as, say, the premières of Meyerbeer's *Robert le diable* and Wagner's *Meistersinger* are more obviously related to structures than are the works on which these events were based. Clearly, the structures of social and cultural history are more useful for explaining why an opera had a spectacular impact with far- reaching repercussions than for trying to fathom the aesthetic essence of a work, as this essence cries out not to be analysed as an event but to be interpreted as a text. In other words, our chances of doing justice to musical occurrences as events in the strong sense rise proportionately as we treat music history as social history – and any social history of music with ambitions to be something more than mere biography marching under the tattered banner of a theory of social milieu must be conceived as a history of the social functions, and not the social origins, of musical works.

The expression 'structural history', which means more than that the structures described are part of the past, might strike us as being suspiciously like a contradiction in terms. After all, a circumstance can be presented as a structure only to the extent that we regard it as impervious to historical change, and conversely we cannot describe it in terms of history until we unravel, or at least loosen, the solid nexus of functions that makes it appear as a system. Furthermore, structural history is said to run the risk of sacrificing historical knowledge proper, i.e. the presentation and explanation of historical processes, to a mania for finding systems, a compulsive urge to make constructs, which derives ultimately from structuralist sociology. In other words, it is uncertain to what extent the structures sought by structural historians can be considered 'ideal types' in Max Weber's sense of the term. Do functional relations existing between the elements of a structure have as much claim to historical reality as the elements themselves? Or is it methodologically justifiable if we mentally complete the torso of reality by taking scattered facts and vague correlations (which may make sense in context but resist empirical verification) and concoct images of the past which are not descriptions but rather constructs – constructs with the function of rendering a fragmentary reality intelligible by demanding special explanations solely for deviations from the ideal type, all non-deviant elements being vouchsafed a meaning by their place in the system?

This first objection, namely that structural history misrepresents historical reality by, as it were, making time stand still, applies not just to modern structural history but also to nineteenth-century cultural history, which found its paradigm in Burckhardt's *Kultur der Renaissance in Italien*. According to Burckhardt, the Renaissance was not a process but a circumstance. However, so long as we regard describing structures as equivalent to devising ideal types, and these ideal types as the tools rather than the results of historical inquiry, there will be progressively less danger of letting our imagined structures loom so large as to overshadow the fact that history is actually a process. If the ideal type primarily serves an heuristic function and helps us to sift the insights that arise by dint of the system from those things that must be understood individually, there is ample leeway for treating occurrences that happen to deviate from or fall outside the system, or that even press for its alteration and, ultimately, its destruction.

Now, the structures that structural historians are at pains to reconstitute are not the same thing as the 'circumstances' spoken of by nineteenth-century historians, their many similarities notwithstanding. Structures are, or at least tend to be, self-contained complexes of functions, whereas circumstances are congeries of loosely connected facts. Admittedly those structures that are empirically intelligible prove to be mere sub-structures, such as the inner workings of the concert system, the categories of aesthetic reception or the technical apparatus of writing music; and though these sub-structures intersect, it is not clear whether, and if so to what extent, they combine to form a 'system of systems' rather than a mere random sampling of sub-structures functioning alongside and through one another. No-one who depicts a 'circumstance' in the nineteenth-century sense would claim to have grasped and illuminated an all-embracing and self-contained system. On the contrary, ample room remains for discrepancies, for divergent facts and, most importantly, for those accidents that intrude upon a functional nexus from the outside. (The ruinous effect of Napoleon's 'Continental System' on London's music life in the early nineteenth century is a fact entirely unconnected with the internal workings of that complex.)

Furthermore, it would seem that the concept 'circumstance' serves as a reminder that systems are always steps within evolutionary processes, and that their foregoing and subsequent stages – which are accessible not through functional analysis but only through historical inquiry – must be taken into account if our understanding is to be complete. Hence it is not at all superfluous to hark back to that somewhat shopsoiled and old-fashioned concept of 'circumstance', as it seems ideally suited to rectifying the onesided aspects of the structural approach. This is not to say that structural history's more ambitious claim of revealing functional complexes rather than arranging facts into a panorama should be sacrificed in favour of a return to the more modest methods of depicting circumstances. But a certain recognition of the advantages of traditional historiography can keep us alive to the limitations we face in our urge to devise systems.

As mentioned above, the concept of a structural history of music stands out in the history of scholarship against the biographical-generical-nationalist approach. But it also offsets that manner of music theory and aesthetics that takes the form of systems, as the historical nature of these systems was largely denied or relegated to the back of the mind in the nineteenth century. We are thus confronted on the one hand by a brand of history lacking a systematic basis and on the other by a set of systems lacking an historical basis. Structural history is an attempt to mediate between the two, i.e. to strike a balance between the depiction of historical states of affairs and the elaboration of theoretical and aesthetic systems by reconstructing the underlying systems of the one and demonstrating the historical coloration and limitations of the other.

Another aim of structural history is the removal of a discrepancy or disproportion that is such a daily matter in music history that we scarcely notice it. Although scholars vying for membership in the musicological guild exercise excruciating care in ferreting out and hoarding individual facts or series of facts, they are nevertheless allowed to utter vague platitudes when defining collective concepts such as 'neo-romanticism' or 'late romanticism' without tarnishing their reputations as they would be getting their numbers wrong or by connecting absurdly contradictory facts. In answer to this inconsistency, structural history – in which a concept such as 'neo-romanticism' would figure as a label for a 'system of systems' – is an attempt to define functions and correlations so as to reach, in the description of large-scale complexes, a degree of precision that may differ in kind from the scrupulous exactitude of fact-finding but which likewise meets the standards set by history as a science, in presentation no less than in research.

A distinction must also be made between structural history and the social history of music, which appears in various guises from the modestly empirical to the ambitiously abstract and philosophical. The difference lies either in the ground they cover or in the methodological principles they apply. In its harmlessly descriptive form, social history is restricted to picturing institutions and social roles, whereas in its Marxist version it proceeds from the axiom that music history as a whole is nothing but a sub-species of social history, being the ideological 'superstructure' to a socio-economic 'base'. Structural history goes beyond the restricted form of social history by including not only institutions and social roles, but also compositional norms and aesthetic ideas, among the elements that go to make up a music-historical structure. (The opposition of structural history to intellectual history, though real, should not be overemphasised. The founders of the structural history method – the historians associated from 1929 with the journal *Annales* – did indeed underscore the significance of economic and socio-historical circumstances and processes; but they never abandoned their interest in intellectual history entirely, as is readily apparent from their discussions of the 'mentality structure' of feudalism.)

Furthermore, structural history differs from the Marxist programme of treating music history as part of social history in that it does without historiological preconceptions. A music historian looking for structures will observe and reconstruct connections or correspondences between economic, social, psychological, aesthetic and compositional facts or chains of facts without deciding *a priori*, before tackling historical details, which strands in the fabric that he views as making up a past music culture are going to be the substantive ones and which the substantiated. To be sure, he reckons with the probable existence of a hierarchy, and does not leave the sifting of essential from inessential facts to the whims of 'cognitive interest'. But he stops short of proclaiming, before examining the facts, how that hierarchy is constituted. That the Marxist thesis may prove to be valid for a number of periods, particularly the nineteenth century, is quite possible, indeed rather likely; but it is in no way a foregone conclusion. Modern structural historians share the Marxists' mistrust of the historicist category 'spirit'. However, unlike the Marxists, they do not simply stand intellectual history on its head and proclaim something else, namely the economic base, to be the real substance of history. Instead they dispense with substances altogether and adopt the formal code of intellectual history, i.e. its function of using a single concept to cover the entirety of connections and interactions between the elements and factors within an historical circumstance. In other words, from the standpoint of methodology, both 'structure' and 'spirit' are categories with the dual task of preventing historical reality from disintegrating into unrelated sub-areas and of letting functional explanations replace the causal ones to which naive social histories tend.

In a manner of speaking, structural history borders on cultural history, as conceived in the eigthteenth and nineteenth centuries, and social history, which has come to the forefront in recent decades. But it differs from them in its methodology, and this difference becomes particularly apparent in relation to the problem of how to write a music history that does equal justice to history and to music. Cultural historians tend automatically to depict history as an imaginary museum, treating the legacy of the past as it appears at first glance from the retrospective vantage point of the present, i.e. as a collection of documents and creations divorced from their original purposes and functions and awaiting aesthetic contemplation. Even tools and implements are turned willy-nilly into *objets d'art*. This is not to say that cultural historians deny the existence of a holistic 'Culture' from which works of art derive; on the contrary, the avowed aim of those 'scenes of yesteryear' (to use the apt title of Gustav Freytag's book *Bilder aus der Vergangenheit*) devised by cultural historians is to reconstruct the context of past art. However, anything functional is so to speak 'aestheticised' and incorporated into the imaginary museum.

Modern social history, on the other hand, attempts just the opposite: musical creations which have been rendered autonomous by the passing of their original environment are restored to the context of social functions that gave rise to them. This manner of history takes as its model, not music that invites aesthetic contemplation, but rather what Besseler would have called 'everyday music' which, being a component of human interaction, represents a social process. Hence, whereas cultural history is in danger of aestheticising the functional and viewing tools as art objects, social history courts the opposite danger of functionalising the aesthetic and mistaking art objects for tools. Structural history seeks to mediate between these two. Nor need structural historians fear cries of eclecticism, for they can always plead that, in reality, music can be and has been both a process and a work, i.e. a component of human interaction and an object of contemplation, and that consequently we must apply our methodological approaches in mixtures of varying strengths to do it proper justice.

The social history of music discredited itself from the very beginning. Faced with the challenge of rendering music – seen as an ideological entity – intelligible and comprehensible in terms of economics, social historians merely harked back to the antiquated aesthetic of expression and biography in order to reconstrue them in sociological terms. To put this as a formula, they deciphered musical forms into expressive content, this content in turn into biography, and finally biography into sociology. Thus they failed to strike out on the only path that might have spelt success, namely leaving music history for the moment to its own devices and testing the viability of the sociological approach on a history of the functions of music. In other words, it is high time to do away with those tiresome disputes in which idealist slogans are forever being turned around and placed on a solid materialist footing – which does not stop them being slogans – and instead to devote ourselves to problems that are not only interesting but can be solved by empirical means. To choose Beethoven as an example, biographies supply anecdotes and a few facts about the 'milieux' in which, and in response to which, he wrote his music, but little to illuminate structures such as the culture of the Viennese nobility around 1800. Nor do we know much about the audience he composed for, even in those cases where he upset or confounded their expectations. Not only do we need to study its social constitution, we must also find out what it expected from music at all, i.e. what functions music fulfilled, or was meant to fulfil. Furthermore, and despite laborious discussions of the terms *Kenner* and *Liebhaber*, we are still ill-informed about the then current level of education in music, i.e. how practical capabilities, aesthetic ideas and social attitudes combined in what were then called the musical 'connoïsseur' and the aristocratic 'dilettante'. And as regards the social role of the composer we cannot even be sure, Beethoven notwithstanding, to what extent the concept 'composer' as we know it today even existed around 1800: Beethoven's position was an exception that today has practically become the rule, but it remains to be seen how the 'rule' that prevailed around 1800 can be determined in sociological terms.

The key category of structural history – the concept of 'correspondence' (also called 'association' or 'complementarity') – did not remain unassailed. For the phenomena brought into correlation by music historians in their search for structures are quite often chronologically out of step with each other (as were, for example, bourgeois concert life and the principle of aesthetic autonomy in the nineteenth century). Indeed, it is probably the exception rather than the rule that they arose and perished at exactly, or even roughly, the same time. Determinations of time remain vague and approximate; and in general the component parts of a system, although they only seemed to acquire significance in their relation to each other, did not emerge simultaneously but coalesced gradually from a number of scattered sources. Consequently, it seldom costs a sceptic mistrustful of the 'structure' concept much effort to show that in any correspondence which appears to be an intrinsically intelligible correlation, the one element preceded or outlived the other. (The institutions of bourgeois concert life antedate the supremacy of the autonomy principle.)

Structural history is put through this ordeal by chronology in order to be seen to fail, as it is bound to do. Yet this test is so rigorous that hardly any principle for the making of historical connections could possibly be expected to pass it. To postulate exactness of association in a discipline that does not construct models but merely outlines types and patterns is absurd and wrongheaded. First of all, there is nothing to prevent things of non-contemporaneous origin from corresponding at a later stage. Phenomena can adapt to a new context by changing in form or function without at the same time sacrificing their identity; and it is also possible, without excess of empirically unredeemable theorising, to distinguish between the duration of a thing and the period to which it 'actually' belongs (though the notion that things have an 'actual' lifespan is controversial, as will be shown later). Secondly, a system of correspondences discovered or devised by the historian as a framework for a period of music history can be taken as an 'ideal type' in Max Weber's sense, i.e. it is meant to be not a mirror likeness of empirical fact but rather a proposal in which we willingly put up with a certain imprecision of time and location in the association of the various parts because the resulting increase of intelligibility outweighs the want of empirical completeness. To be sure, arguments can arise in scholarly practice over the criteria for deciding whether or not the empirical grounding is adequate. Moreover an historian must always be ready to find in his period not only correspondences but discrepancies as well, at times even unintelligible discrepancies. Any attempt to present the musical culture of an age in its entirety, with no loose ends, as a structure or a structure of structures would be misguided and presumptuous. Besides facts that fall into line with the system there will inevitably be isolated, recalcitrant facts that will not. And though historians, being descendants of storytellers, have a natural inclination to make the past intelligible by integrating wayward facts into an unbroken continuity, we must not forget that alongside connected facts there will invariably be unrelated ones as well. (Schumann and Donizetti, or Liszt and Offenbach, though enticingly contemporary, simply will not brook comparison.)

The most difficult and intractable problem for structural history, and an almost paralysing one, is the so-called 'non-contemporaneity of the contemporaneous'. At present it is not even clear just what this much-cited phenomenon means in methodological terms – which historiographical consequences it admits and which it compels. The structures (be they institutions, modes of thought or patterns of behaviour) that coexist at any given time, interacting to constitute or determine an historical circumstance, differ from each other not only in respect of their age, i.e. how far back they extend into the past and the timespan allotted to them, but also in the rate at which they alter. Fernand Braudel, a member of the *Annales* circle, spoke of the various 'rhythms' of coexisting structures, ranging from the geographic conditions of a culture to the styles of its art. And, to use a musical metaphor, there is cause to doubt whether the overlapping tempos can be reduced to a common underlying metre (though Wilhelm Pinder felt that succession of generations formed a certain 'natural rhythm' to the history of art). Using Aristotle's definition of time as the measure of motion there is, strictly speaking, no such thing as 'Time' in the singular – a homogeneous medium binding events of various durations and rates of change – but only 'times' in the plural, the times of overlapping structures in conflicting rhythms.

The heterogeneity of the 'rhythms' that Braudel spoke of in reference to geographic conditions, social structures, political constitutions and fashions in clothing can even be observed within a field as narrow as music history. Not only are the 'rhythms' that underly some of the essential elements of music in our century – e.g. inventions such as the radio, gramophone disc or recording tape, musical institutions such as the opera or concert, the changes in compositional technique or our conception of music – at variance with each other, they are quite obviously unrelated. We can describe what the overlapping produces at a given time, but we still lack a conclusive argument to justify our choice of one 'rhythm' rather than another for marking out periods in twentieth-century music.

Besides what we might call the 'formal' difficulty of preventing us from proclaiming one of the several contesting 'rhythms' as the real, fundamental measure for the course of 'History', the non-contemporaneity of the contemporaneous harbours a problem as regards meaning or content. How, without being arbitrary, can we decide just which of the events and structures coexisting at a given time are genuinely in line with the *Zeitgeist* and can hence serve as a gauge for determining whether other, 'non-contemporaneous', phenomena are by comparison 'earlier' or 'later'? Are historical facts 'non-contemporaneous' in some ever-shifting relation to one another, or do some of them represent things whose 'time has come' while others stand out by being 'untimely'? Histories of musical styles and genres proceed from the organism model, which conveys the impression that the point which comes closest to the *Zeitgeist* is the middle life of a genre, style or generation, i.e. the age at which, in the language of eighteenth-century philosophy of history, a *point de la perfection* has been reached. Older generations or styles, on the other hand, merely 'survive' but are no longer actually current, while younger generations or new styles have already 'set to work' or 'announced their arrival' without actually being of immediate import. Yet in many periods, such as the *Sturm und Drang*, romanticism and expressionism, the *Zeitgeist* almost seems to have been usurped by the younger generation, which casts considerable confusion on the use of the generation model as a basis for writing art history. And assuming that we can withstand the lure of historiological schemes that claim metaphysical priority for one evolutionary stage or another, we might even think that we should dispense altogether with accepting or hypostatising the existence of a *Zeitgeist*, because all that empirical studies ever reveal is a series of overlapping structures in irreconcilably conflicting 'rhythms' and at various stages in their own internal development, none of these stages being more 'substantive' than any other. (Whatever applies to the *Zeitgeist* can just as easily be said of the socio-economic structure, which is merely the *Zeitgeist* set the right way up for us by the Marxists.)

As might be expected, the very same dispute over hierarchy among those economic, social, psychological, aesthetic and compositional factors that impinge on music history crops up again in the controversy over the methodological repercussions of the non-contemporaneity of the contemporaneous, albeit in a new formulation. Namely, we face the choice of conceding priority to the economic base either wholesale or in individual cases; and assuming we make economics our final arbiter, we can either choose relative autonomy as our historiographical principle or find it expedient to call upon the arbiter incessantly, thereby letting music history be subsumed into the totality of social history. And depending on our choice, i.e. depending on which side we take, theoretically and practically, in the controversy over the relative autonomy of music history, our opinions will vary on two questions: does it make sense to personify chronology, as it were, into a *Zeitgeist*; and, assuming that this *Zeitgeist* does exist, where are we most likely to pin it down?

In principle, the significance that can attach to contemporaneity among historical phenomena runs a full gamut. At the one extreme phenomena can be utterly unrelated (e.g. chronological coincidence is irrelevant to history if the events occurred in cultures with no points of contact whatsoever); at the other they betray the obvious presence of a *Zeitgeist* pervading all areas of a culture with equal force. In the first case chronology is of no matter; in the second events receive their meaning according to the moment of their occurrence. However, there is no call for historians to feel pressured into choosing *a priori* between one or the other of these extremes. In the daily business of writing history it is more important to bear historiological problems in mind than to come down in favour of a particular solution. It is quite enough to recall that even though it is an illegitimate metaphyiscal preconception to posit a necessary substantive link between all the things that happened at the same time, there is still nothing to prevent us from trying to discover an intelligible pattern in the different 'rhythms' and 'life stages' of structures that happened to coincide in the past, rather than meekly capitulating in the face of a chaos of contradictory facts. Indeed, the very fact that we can describe the coincidence and interplay of structures such as institutions, ideas and behavioural norms as an historical 'circumstance' at all (always assuming that we are dealing with systems in contact with one another and not, as in the case of Chinese and European cultures before the seventeenth century, with completely unconnected ones) is a clear indication that we also stand some chance of understanding them as a circumstance with an underlying order, i.e. to a certain extent as a structure of structures.

Suppose we wanted, by way of example, to sketch the categorical framework of a music culture, say that of Central Europe in the nineteenth century, excluding opera. We can choose our starting point at random, firstly because any point in the system is reachable from any other, and secondly because a description of connections and correspondences does not *prima facie* say anything about a hierarchy of sub-elements. Therefore, it should not be misconstrued and deplored as an 'idealist' preconception if we start by assuming the principle of aesthetic autonomy, i.e. the right of artificial music to be listened to for its own sake rather than serve a function within an overriding extramusical process.

So obviously is the autonomy principle connected with the aesthetic of genius and the concept of originality on the one hand and (in curious contrast) with the mercantile nature of music on the other, that there is no reason to labour the point here. Furthermore, this connection of substance is likewise one of chronology, the decisive changes having taken place in the latter part of the eighteenth century. Nonetheless there is some difficulty in finding the proper emphasis. However illuminating the thesis of the fundamental significance of economics may be – and even non-Marxists are convinced of its applicability to the nineteenth century – it runs into difficulties when confronted by the throng of historical details. Firstly, it is not clear that the mercantile nature of art entirely dominated the concept of works. Composition made up only a small portion of the economic existence of nineteenth-century composers: not even traditional court positions had entirely disappeared in the 'age of the bourgeoisie', and (in contradistinction to their influence in the seventeenth and eighteenth centuries) such socio-economic dependency as they occasioned had little if any influence on the works composed. (Works written to commission degenerated into *parerga*.) Secondly, the law governing music as a commodity – namely the compulsion to be original so as to stand out, and then to exploit the resultant success by self-imitation – applies only in part to artificial music. Self-imitation was shunned as a breach of the originality principle, which required of composers not only that they compose 'from within' but that they be innovative. This is not to say that the foregoing arguments imply the primacy of the autonomy principle over socio-economic reality, of ideals over interests; but at the least they suffice to show that the web of dependencies is more tangled than orthodox Marxist doctrine allows.

The institution that corresponds to the autonomy principle is bourgeois concert life. Building on eighteenth-century origins, the concert system fully established itself during the post-Napoleonic restoration from 1815 and reached a form closest to its 'ideal type' around mid century with the incorporation of esoteric chamber music into public concerts and the exclusion of 'trivial' elements from symphony programmes. Now, once we concede that artificial music, being (to quote Hanslick) the outward manifestation of 'spirit in spiritually tractable matter', exists to be listened to for its own sake, it follows that the only appropriate way of receiving it is that form of aesthetic contemplation so penetratingly described by Schopenhauer. And in fact aesthetic contemplation did eventually become standard behaviour at concerts, and later even at the opera. We need not deny the existence of the sociable and ceremonial sides of concert life, or the pleasure taken in displays of virtuosity, or the bourgeoisie's compulsion for self-display, to maintain that the ideal of aesthetic autonomy was the crucial development in nineteenth-century music, and that it took hold with no recognisable economic motives. It was under the banner of this

development that, in the mid nineteenth century, strict aes-
theticism became the norm in the concert repertory, as typified by
the transformation of the solo concert into the 'symphony' concert.

The aesthetic imperatives contained in the autonomy principle
found a correlate in a complex of compositional techniques.
Among the distinguishing characteristics of this complex are (1) the
self-sufficiency of instrumental music (i.e. its emancipation from
extramusical ends and from having to function as an introduction or
interlude); (2) the form-giving properties of tonal harmony (the
discovery that tonality can impart inner cohesion to large-scale
forms by purely musical means, without texts or programmes); and
(3) thematic and motivic manipulation, or 'developing variation',
to use Schoenberg's term. Music designed to be listened to for its
own sake took the form of what Johann Mattheson called a
'discourse in sound', i.e. an acoustical rendering of a logic at work
both in the key structure and in the interplay of theme and motive.
(The term 'musical logic', apparently coined by J. N. Forkel, was a
fundamental concept of the age.) Music, therefore, gives the
imperatives of the autonomy principle their due by means of logic
in the closely allied phenomena of key and motive, and thereby
vindicates the aesthetic *hubris* which many observers saw in the
emancipation of instrumental music from the mid eighteenth century onwards. Today we take it for granted that music has a right to
exist even if it expresses neither a text nor a programme, is useless
for dancing and kindles no astonishment at its virtuosity. Around
1800, however, this view was considered something of a paradox.
(It is particularly revealing that the proponents of musical hermeneutics were fond of fabricating tacit programmes in order to
explain away the puzzling aspects of what E. T. A. Hoffmann
called 'pure instrumental music'.)

Aesthetic autonomy as understood by the nineteenth-century
bourgeoisie is by no means equivalent to the principle of art for
art's sake, which in fact was a catchphrase of the bohemian sub-
culture rather than of the bourgeois establishment. Far from imply-
ing the isolation of music, aesthetic autonomy meant just the
opposite, namely that music played an active part in one of the
main currents of the age: the notion of *Bildung*, or liberal education and the cultivation of the mind. As conceived by Fichte and
Wilhelm von Humboldt, *Bildung* presupposes or occasions an
inner detachment from everyday utilitarian matters and spiritual
liberation from the 'dictates of necessity'. Accordingly music,
being what Ludwig Tieck called a 'world separate unto itself' and

hence an object of aesthetic contemplation, can become a means for freeing oneself from the socio-economic pressures of daily life. Precisely by being autonomous, art represents an alternative authority to the phenomenon of alienation, of which Humboldt was to speak a full half-century before Marx. In its function as an alternative world to the 'realm of necessity', the 'free art' of the bourgeoisie carried on the legacy of the *ars liberalis*, that manner of philosophic contemplation that was born in Antiquity of the leisure of the aristocracy, of their freedom from household cares.

As mentioned above, the autonomy principle was closely allied to the aesthetic of genius and the notion of originality, both survivals from the late eighteenth century. Not only was autonomous music vindicated in a formal and aesthetic sense by musical logic, it also received a philosophical legitimation – a 'necessity for existing', to use Novalis's phrase – by being a product of genius. Artificial music thus demands double duty of its listeners, asking them not only to 'retrace' the musical logic of the work in their minds but at the same time to project themselves into the personality and originality of the composer. This dual claim on the listener merges into the concept of *Verstehen* in music, a nineteenth-century category that vacillated between intellectual reconstruction and spiritual empathy. An entire aesthetic of reception for the age could have turned on this concept. As it was, this aesthetic was never committed to paper during the age itself. (Today it is a commonplace to speak of 'understanding' pure instrumental music instead of merely finding it agreeable, but around 1800 this view was somewhat paradoxical.)

Now, according to prevailing opinion in the nineteenth century, to say that the essence of genius consisted in radical originality means two things. Firstly, provided that a piece of music is 'poetic' rather than 'prosaic' – which in Schumann's aesthetic is equivalent to saying that it has not been banished from the domain of art by reason of its triviality, whether of the frivolous or the academic variety – the composer is using the piece to express himself. (This principle of expression was sometimes interpreted crudely to mean that the aesthetic ego and the day-to-day empirical ego are identical, with the consequence that works of music were construed as fragments from a biography in notes.) Secondly, it implies that if a composer wishes his music to be heard in those circles whose opinion matters he has to say something new. From the eighteenth century onwards, aesthetics has decreed (though at times with violent opposition from some parts of the public) that if music is to be authentic it must be innovative. And without being historiologically high-handed we can easily recognise in this demand for innovation that same idea of progress that was felt to be the mainstay of the early industrial age.

Yet the idea of progress was not alone in determining the aesthetic thought of the age. It also worked in conjunction with the veneration of genius, i.e. with the thesis that products of genius stand apart from history. Starting with the concept of the 'classical' work – a concept that only took hold in music aesthetics from 1800, centuries after it had made its way into literary theory – there gradually emerged, in interaction with increasing difficulties of performance, a fixed concert repertory with Beethoven's symphonies at its core. In one way this codification of the repertory represents an alternative authority and an obstacle to the novelty postulate; but in another way, as disparagers of the 'musical museum' fail to note, it can also come to the support of that postulate. We must distinguish between qualitative novelty, as demanded in the nineteenth century, and merely chronological novelty, which was taken for granted in the eighteenth century. As long as a piece of music had to make sense at first hearing, as was the case in the eighteenth century when there was little chance of its ever being repeated, to be radically innovative was deliberately to court failure. Only when a work is given the opportunity of being performed again, on the off-chance that its initial incomprehensibility might betoken genius and make the work eligible for future inclusion in the repertory, does it become practicable for a composer to venture far-reaching or challenging innovations. Radical progressivism goes hand in hand with expectations of future classical status, as is most evident in the case of Wagner.

Thus the musical repertory emerged from the idea of the 'classical' work towering above history. As a consequence, the music of the past, even of the very remote past, presented itself to nineteenth-century composers in the form of individual works rather than general norms. Composers learnt norms as before, but they were no longer of paramount importance. Of course a seventeenth-century adept of composition studied earlier works too, but he understood them (to put it bluntly) not as unique creations but as instances exemplifying a norm. The fragments from Palestrina offertories that Christoph Bernhard included in his treatise on composition were meant to be *exempla classica*, and served an entirely different function from Beethoven's Ninth, which Wagner wrote out with the intention of making a composer of himself. Art, as understood in the romantic period, was not a craft based on rules as exemplified in the great masterpieces. Rather, it was a realm of which the composer partook (or from which he was excluded): the realm of the 'poetic'. The masterpieces which made up the repertory, or at least the ideal repertory, intimated the existence of this realm, but imitation of them was strictly prohibited.

This decline in the prestige accorded to rules of craftsmanship was closely allied to a decline in the importance of traditional genres. Previously, musical genres had come into being, to put it in formulaic terms, as a congruence between a social function and a compositional norm, i.e. between an extramusical end to be served and the musical means available for and appropriate to its fulfilment (what was permitted in a madrigal might be anathema in a motet). It was this nexus of 'external' social function and 'internal' musical technique which tradition handed down to later composers as the essence of their craft. In the nineteenth century, by contrast, functionality in music was either obliterated entirely or relegated to the backstairs of music by the principle of aesthetic autonomy. Furthermore, the authority of generic norms in composition was challenged by the aesthetic presence of individual works. This is not to say that it did not matter what genre a work belonged to (this development had to wait until our century); but genre became a secondary distinguishing characteristic of works of art conceived primarily as self-sufficient entities and not as exemplary instances.

The aesthetics of genius as an alternative authority to a poetics of music proceeding from norms; the autonomy principle that suppressed or vitiated functionality in music; *Bildung* as a correlate to aesthetic autonomy; the category of musical *Verstehen* with its double burden of retracing musical logic and empathising with the personality and originality of the composer; bourgeois concert life as an institutionalisation of the ideal of autonomy and yet, in radical contrast, as a manifestation of mercantilism in music; the emancipation of instrumental music; the presence of classical works standing beyond the confines of history and forming a fixed repertory in precarious relation to the postulate of innovation and the ideal of progress; the veneration of originality as something to be sought but not emulated; the jeopardising of the traditional musical genres; and lastly the stressing of the 'poetical' and denigration of the 'mechanical' (which was felt to be either self-evident or beneath notice) – all of these took form in the nineteenth century as discrete, complementary, mutually derivative sub-elements of one and the same musical 'circumstance', as characteristics of a musical culture which, with the chronological licence normally allowed in the construction of ideal types, lends itself to description as a structure of structures.

10

Problems in reception history

There has been a noticeable, at times even polemical and propagandistic, upsurge of interest in what is called the history of 'impact' or 'reception' (the former term emphasises the object that sets the process in motion, the latter the public towards which that process is directed). This turn of events can be seen as an outgrowth and consequence of the crisis which, beginning in art itself and later moving to art theory, has befallen the concept of the autonomous and self-contained work. We might even yield to the current argot of the subject and say that the authority of the art work has atrophied in an age imprinted with the thought processes of ideology critique. As long as a musical creation was still considered an 'ideal object' with an immutable and unshifting 'real' meaning, whether or not this meaning had been fully or even partly comprehended, reception history seemed at best a secondary venture, if not altogether superfluous. The point was to find the interpretation that could lay sole claim to absolute verity, not to explain why most interpretations were inadequate. There was little sense in reflecting on the historical conditions behind the varying interpretations given to a work of art when the task at hand was to unveil the material content or truths that dwelt, or were thought to dwell, within it. Conflicting views were studied not for their causes but for their cogency. The context of discovery gave way to the context of aesthetic validation: no longer were the component parts of a work gradually combined to yield a pure and unalloyed understanding; instead, the work's meaning – which exists *a priori* even if imperfectly understood at first – was suddenly revealed in undiminished splendour, its separate components having fallen perfectly into place. (The criterion used for judging an interpretation was whether, having coincided with surviving evidence on the composer's intentions, it struck a satisfactory balance between complexity and coherence.)

It is an almost standard complaint levelled at past music histories that they suppressed or neglected the history of reception. This complaint is wide of the mark, and probably resulted from an urge on the part of the complainers to create a foil against which their own scholarly programme might stand out in greater relief. In the first place, one theme of 'impact' history has always been a central concern of music historians, namely the influence of earlier pieces of music on later ones. Indeed, in some histories what we might call 'reception as practised by composers' is practically the only thread connecting works which otherwise, being art works in the strong sense (i.e. aesthetic objects contemplated in isolation), would constantly be at loggerheads. Secondly, the problem does not lie in whether certain facts are being ignored but in how these facts are interpreted. No-one has ever denied or overlooked the fact that works of music have been viewed differently at different times and under different circumstances. The problem is that these changes used to be seen in relation to an 'ideal object' which a work was thought to represent, i.e. they were taken as approximations of a 'real' meaning which might perhaps never be fully disclosed but still represented a goal to be attained by various means. As long as this notion of a single interpretation valid for all times and pursued by various routes was still untarnished by scepticism there seemed to be little value in studying the historical preconditions to these varying degrees of approximation. Not until the notion of a pre-existent, objective *a priori* body of material content or truths has been done away with and a change has been wrought in the meaning of the works themselves, rather than in the manner and accuracy with which that meaning is approximated, do the historical conditions behind the changing modes of reception become basic and indispensable to the study of music history. The final arbiter will then no longer be the concept 'work', which reception historians reject, but 'moment in history', i.e. the forces that condition reception. And it is to this final arbiter that we must turn to understand how a work has 'meaning' at all, a meaning not contained within an abstract text but one which takes concrete form, and in turn 'concretises' the text, only in the course of reception.

Thus, thanks to the aesthetics of reception the 'ideal object' theory, which attributed meaning to works independently of the comprehension or lack of comprehension of an actual public, has largely fallen into disrepute. This is hardly surprising in an age in which the very word 'metaphysics' has become a philosophical term of abuse. Nowadays the traditional aesthetic of works can be justified, if at all, only in terms of heuristics (not metaphysics), namely by arguing that any interpreter with ambitions to be an historian will have to make himself the medium primarily of works and their claim to be heard as art rather than of his own place in history and the prejudices of the times. If the aesthetic of works runs the risk of being an illusion conjured up by a discarded metaphysic, reception history faces the danger of smallmindedness: having realised that he can never entirely escape the assumptions that underlie and delimit his own age, the reception historian is tempted to draw, half from resignation and half from presumption, the dubious conclusion that, since he can never completely neutralise his prejudices anyway, he might as well immure himself in them deliberately and conduct his *studia humanitatis* as it were from the standpoint of ignorance – to use outdated expressions for something that can scarcely be articulated in the language of today.

For most adherents of reception history and its associated aesthetic, the provocative claim made by extreme relativists that there are as many Eroica symphonies as there are listeners in our concert halls is less a confession they feel compelled to make than an awkward consequence they fully intend to avoid. Felix V. Vodička, for instance, has repudiated not only 'dogmatism', i.e. the positing of an ideal existence for the message of a work, but 'subjectivism' as well, meaning the disintegration of the identity of a work into countless individual reactions. Instead he argues in favour of a middle path. On the one hand he would like 'in general to have several aesthetic, content-related interpretations coexist for a given work, with each one in principle having equal validity and cogency, however restricted to particular periods, societies and, to a certain extent, individuals'.[1] On the other hand he maintains that the object of reception history does not lie in individual reactions but in norms and normative systems that determine how surviving texts are perceived within groups or strata conditioned by history, society and ethnic origin. Admittedly Vodička leaves unanswered the question as to how different, mutually exclusive interpretations can coexist with equal rights and not undermine the identity of the work – and in his discussion of Roman Ingarden's writings he forgets that it was precisely this problem of identity that Ingarden took as his starting point. Even so, Vodička's proposed methodology does represent a realisable programme, unlike the theses of extreme subjectivism, which were evidently spawned more from a desire to

[1] 'Die Konkretisation des literarischen Werks', p. 90.

destroy metaphysics than in order to function as a plan of action for history.

In Hans Robert Jauss's view, the process of 'concretisation' whereby literary texts (and by analogy musical ones as well) become aesthetic objects should not be taken onesidedly to mean either the impact of the work or its reception in categories determined by the observer. Instead, the process has the structure of what he calls an 'intersubjective dialogue':

The process of transmitting the impact and reception of a work of art consists in a dialogue between a present-day subject and a past subject. In this dialogue, the past subject will be in a position to 'say something' to the other (or, as Gadamer would put it, to say something meant for him and him alone) only if this present-day subject recognises the answer implicit in the earlier discourse as also applying to a question that he himself must pose ('Racines und Goethes Iphigenie', p. 348).

Quite apart from the fact that there is not always a subject speaking in art works of the past, another difficulty lurks in the notion of a 'question that [the present-day subject] himself must pose'. Either (following Collingwood's dictum that to understand a text means to apprise oneself of the question it is meant to answer) a question posed by the text in its original meaning has retained, or regained, its topical import; or conversely the interpreter must start from the assumption that any question arising in the present will be aesthetically warranted, whether or not it is historically legitimate, so long as the text that 'answers' it preserves sufficient unity and coherence and does not disintegrate into contradictory or unrelated pieces (though it should be noted that the criteria of 'coherence' vary according to the preconditions of the style concerned, whether classicist or mannerist).

'Quidquid recipitur, recipitur ad modum recipientis.' (Whatever is perceived is perceived according to the manner of the perceiver.) However, to belabour a text with questions is not in itself sufficient to bring it from silence to speech. Reception historians may claim that a text will not speak of its own accord, but this only provokes the rejoinder that texts will give confused answers, or no answer at all, to ill-conceived questions. The real difficulty lies in individual instances, i.e. in deciding to what extent an interpretation must be supported and conditioned by the claims of the work as art on the one hand and by the minds of the recipients on the other if it is to be not simply legitimate but also vital.

Thus, while reception historians incline by their very nature to distrust the distinction between appropriate and ill-conceived views of musical works, they are nevertheless reluctant to dispense entirely with criteria for selecting and classifying modes of reception lest they find themselves adrift in a sea of relativism. Nor is it a foregone conclusion that a history of reception is a process that lends itself to narration at all, rather than a mere accumulation of data that fall into no discernible pattern. These twin problems of how to substantiate opinions and how to cast changing modes of reception into coherent history are intimately connected.

One starting point for the reception historian lies in the proposition that the criterion for judging competing views of a work does not reside in how close they come to its alleged 'real meaning', but rather how accurately, subtly and intensely they represent the age, the nation, and the class or social group which conditioned them. In other words, the key issue is not reconstruction of the past so much as construction in the spirit of the present. In point of methodology it is of no great importance whether a reception history of this sort is geared primarily to intellectual or to social history, notwithstanding the grave political and philosophical differences between the two, for in both approaches the main historiographical focus is not the musical work but the intellectual or social structure – what Vodička would call the normative system – that supplied a context for the work's reception. Seen in this light, the history of music reception is a part of intellectual or social history. True, it takes its material mainly from documentary evidence of how pieces of music were received. But its structure, seen from the vantage point of music history, is heteronomous: it owes its internal coherence as a narrative history to a continuity which, being borrowed from intellectual or social history, remains practically untouched by musical facts.

This criterion of historical representation proves its worth as a standard for selection and as a guiding principle for casting changing modes of reception into a form deserving of the name history. Its price, however, is the notion that interpretations of a work correspond to its real meaning. Instead, meaning is sought in an affinity to the spirit of the age in which the interpretation originated or gained ascendency. We might almost speak of the 'historical' as opposed to the 'material' adequacy of an interpretation, with the former rooted in the historical situation and the latter pertaining to the work alone. Still, the sacrifice we must make when we elevate historical representation to our paramount criterion is considerable, being nothing less than the identity of works of art. Henceforth a surviving musical creation represents nothing more than an acoustical substrate, an auditory phenomenon that only becomes music at all by means of a categorical process which proves to be variable and interchangeable in its most significant features (reception history would consign itself to irrelevance if these historical changes were assumed to be limited to secondary features).

But the identity of works is not irrevocably doomed. We can salvage it by upholding the distinction between appropriate and ill-conceived conceptions of works, i.e. by subscribing to the customary view (so remarkably resistent to theoretical sophistry) that a work of music does have a precise meaning (at least in its most essential aspects, if not absolutely) which may or may not be brought to light by a particular interpretation. On the other hand, this saddles us with the difficulty of having to find a fixed point from which to make well-founded pronouncements as to how near an interpretation is to the 'real' material content of a work. In fact, it turns out that each of the positions we have to choose from harbours philosophical implications that add a touch of speculation to reception history, for all its avowed intentions to proceed along strictly empirical lines.

Now, this 'real meaning' which we posit for works so as to preserve their identity, reducing historical representation to a secondary matter in the process, need not be present or recognisable from the outset. Many reception historians assume, without thereby sacrificing the identity principle, that the present represents only a temporary goal in the subsequent history of a work, during which the work undergoes changing, complementary and mutually corrective interpretations, both in words and in performances, which continually disclose or highlight new traits. And it is through this process that a work comes into its own, that is inner potential unfolds into reality. Thus what Walter Benjamin called the 'after-life' of art works would seem to refer to the evolution of their inner truths, which, especially in major works, remain largely latent at first and only gradually come to light, or which do not attach to a work at all except in the later stages of its reception. It follows that the identity of a work resides in the continuity of its subsequent history and in the goal of a complete and perfect interpretation to which this history aspires, and which, perhaps, must remain forever out of reach.

This line of argument proposes that the subsequent history of musical works consists in the gradual unfolding of their meaning, at least in the case of significant works (and there is a perfectly legitimate hermeneutic circle at work between the two categories of 'significance' in aesthetics and 'unfolding of meaning' in reception history). But this thesis must face an antithesis, namely that insofar as works express or reflect the spirit of their times they are best understood at the time they were written. These two propositions have equally sound philosophical pedigrees and equal claims to be applied in practice, but they stand in glaring, uncompromising contrast to one another. Historians have long been convinced that the only way to arrive at an appropriate and undistorted understanding of a work lies in reconstructing the categories and opinions of contemporary listeners. Yet, firmly ingrained as it is, this conviction would be ruinous for reception history if it was left unchallenged. For the later history of a work would suffer more or less the fate that befalls it when art works are treated as 'ideal objects'; in both instances later reception becomes, not an object of study, but mere rubble to be carted away in order to get to the actual point of the matter, the work in its ideal or original state.

Since these two views are more metaphysical than empirical in origin we have little difficulty in recognising in them the same rough and ready schemata into which philosophies of history are sometimes classified: the schema of progress, and the schema of decline. To claim that only contemporary listeners (and a few historians who are capable of turning themselves into contemporaries in their imagination) can properly understand a work is tantamount to saying that the subsequent history of a work is one of alienation and decline, in which the possibility of restoration exists but the possibility of surpassing the original state does not. We are left only with an unhappy choice between stagnation and regression. The opposite holds true of the belief that, in the case of works that tower above their times, later interpretations tend, at least potentially, to be more rewarding than earlier ones since the meaning of a work unfolds only in the course of its later history. This belief is unmistakably nourished on the idea of progress, which has as it were sought refuge in reception history after increasingly losing currency in the history of composition.

There is a third historiological schema in the thought that neither the start nor the 'temporary goal' of a work's subsequent history represents a state of relative completion, but rather that this history proceeds from rudimentary and tentative beginnings toward what eighteenth-century philosophers of history called a *point de la perfection*, thereafter declining from this state or stagnating within it. Now, however scant its influence on current notions as to what constitutes reception history, this view would seem to suit a good many phenomena. Thus, for instance, the later history of Beethoven's Ninth evidently culminated in the mid nineteenth century when this work became the quintessence of the symphony, not only influencing Wagner, Bruckner and Brahms but even serving as the subject of a novel, Wolfgang Griepenkerl's *Die Beethovener*. Similarly, one could speak of the 1920s as being a *kairos* in the reception of Bruckner's symphonies, i.e. the point at which their 'time had come'; and it is not unthinkable that the years around 1970 might someday represent the high-water mark in the later history of Mahler's works.

This attempt to extract a principle for music historiography from the notion of an historical *kairos*, thereby skirting the straightforward schemes of progress and decline, could have far-reaching consequences, which apparently have yet to be sketched, even though a closer inspection reveals them to be more plausible than not. A history of music with a chronological framework based less on dates of composition than on dates of reception (though admittedly these latter, like dates in structural history, are vague and imprecise) would place Bach's works at various points in the nineteenth century (depending on their genre), Schubert's late symphonies in the middle of the same century, Wagner's *Ring* during the heyday of Bayreuth around the turn of the century, and Charles Ives's posthumous oeuvre in the 1960s. Strictly speaking, it was not the rediscovery of the St Matthew Passion that took place in 1829 but its discovery. Bach's works, in their original form, were relegated to an existence on the sidelines of history; it was not until they were reinterpreted as autonomous music in the nineteenth century that they unfolded into works of an historical significance that was denied them in the eighteenth century, when they stood in the shadow of Telemann. The amazing thing is that they withstood this reinterpretation and without it might never have come into their own as works of art. The fact that Bach's works could become the paradigm of a concept of art that they did not originally partake of is an historiologically baffling, almost monstrous occurrence. The history of eighteenth-century music can, as Handschin claimed, be written with barely a mention of Bach, or with no mention at all, notwithstanding his influence on his son Emmanuel; this is unthinkable in a history of nineteenth-century music.

The idea of a *kairos* or *point de la perfection* in the reception history of musical works may smack somewhat of speculative metaphysics and puzzle historians whose consciences are troubled by any attempt to persuade them to leave, even for an instant, the comfortable ground of empiricism. However, the claim that Bruckner's symphonies reached their historical consummation in the 1920s – and this not merely in a superficial statistical sense but in an intrinsic sense as reflected in commentaries and analyses – is not exclusively normative. It can also be construed heuristically. In this case, it should not be taken as an attempt to turn a particular stage in the interpretation of Bruckner into a dogma and let it stand outside history as an authority from which to pronounce judgment on other periods. Instead it means simply that the insights of the 1920s form a useful vantage point for surveying this historical process in its entirety and rendering it intelligible. Even if it is impossible to conceive these insights now (several decades later and in a quite different historical situation), they nevertheless remain comprehensible and recognisable in their significance. For the moment at least we can entirely suspend their normative claim, which empiricists find so suspect, without also having to discard the categories and viewpoints gained by analysis of what we intuitively feel is the culminating stage in the reception of Bruckner. Indeed, these categories form both the preconditions and a solid basis for comparing the other stages. Without them, these stages would not be describable at all as part of a coherent historical development, but would appear merely as adjuncts to changing conditions within intellectual and social history.

The proposition that some ways of receiving a given work are more to the point than others has been questioned by sceptics who feel they are being empiricists when they attribute 'in principle . . . equal validity and power of conviction' (Vodička) to any view of a piece that can be historically documented – as though equality of rights were not just as firmly rooted in value-decisions as inequality. In fact, all that empiricism tells us is that opinions differ in the material content they reveal, in the social strata that sustain them, and in their power, or lack of power, to compel conviction. Obviously this power varies, and any claim that opinions nevertheless have equal rights is clearly motivated by ethical or metaphysical considerations.

In these competing principles for distinguishing appropriate from ill-conceived modes of reception we can detect some of the same moral tenets that have been at work in political histories of the last few centuries. However, the fact that the two are connected does not imply that the one is reducible to the other: within the historical sciences it is more important to discover connections and correlations than to dispute what ultimately caused what, as these disputes almost invariably arise from ulterior motives. The arbiters called upon to legitimate historical and aesthetic opinions as to whether a mode of reception is appropriate or not include, briefly, (1) the origin of an interpretation, (2) the extent to which it illuminates the phenomenon in question, (3) the number of people who believe in it, and (4) the aforementioned principle that all interpretations enjoy equal status. (Vodička's focus on group rather than individual opinion may temper the relativism to which his thesis naturally tends, but it does not free him from it: basically, the mere existence of a mode of reception still constitutes its *raison d'être*.)

Any historian who appeals to the intentions of a composer, or to the prevailing opinion of the audience that first heard a work, manifestly accepts the origins of a view as a seal of its authenticity without necessarily being aware of the moral and political affinities of his value-decision. No matter how scant and insufficient a composer's or his contemporaries' interpretation of a work may seem to him, he will still take great pains not to exchange a traditional view of a work for his own, and would rather ride roughshod over his aesthetic sensibilities than offend his historical conscience. The latter-day historian lives in mortal fear of the anachronism and arrogance that seem to lurk in the disparagement of 'authentic' opinions – as though to discredit them would be to sin against the spirit of the whole enterprise of history.

The objections that have been levelled in hermeneutic disputes against what we might call the 'authority principle' just outlined are so familiar that it is enough to recall them here without further comment. Firstly, even if external sources directly or indirectly document the intentions of a composer, their relevance is not always assured, for a composer (to put it crudely) does not have to know what he is doing. Secondly, assuming that a composer has realised his intention in a work (and unrealised intentions are beside the point), there are still no criteria for distinguishing this intention from an interpretation advanced by an historian which is equally in harmony with the received text. Lastly, it is specious metaphysics to claim that a connection with a common *Zeitgeist* is sufficient grounds for giving privileged historiological status to a view of a work that was held by its original public; to the dispassionate observer documents on contemporary reactions or statements from composers as to their professed intentions are nothing more than material for the historian, and they are not the final arbiter of his interpretation.

The tradition or 'authority' principle can be replaced to a certain extent, in a political and moral sense, by a principle of 'cogency', namely by advancing the counter-proposal that any interpretation which discloses a higher degree of complexity and, at the same time, of integration and unity in a work, without doing violence to the text, thereby proves itself superior to rival interpretations, regardless of where it came from or what historical conditions (which may well differ from those that obtained when the work was composed) made it possible. In other words, the 'real' meaning of a work of music is determined, not by the opinions of its composer or of the social stratum for which it was originally written, but by the interpretation that achieves the greatest possible cogency as measured against the aesthetic criteria of diversity and inner coherence. History and tradition step down in favour of aesthetics and structure as the sources of legitimacy.

The prevalence of a view or mode of reception is a criterion that an aesthetician may well deplore as crude and banal, but no historian should ignore or delude himself about the extent of its influence. Even cultists are fond of disseminating at least rumours of the cause they espouse, if not the cause itself. Nevertheless, we will never be able to assess the consequences of popular success for the writing of music history until we distinguish between success in performance, which can be measured, and the impact of prestige, which cannot. Prestige can be the lengthened shadow of a long-forgotten successful performance (Mendelssohn's *St Paul*), it can arise independently of success in performance (Bach's *Art of Fugue*), transcend that success (Wagner's *Parsifal*) or even foretell it (Berlioz' *Les troyens*). Without delving into the dizzying interplay of categories involved we can at least make some general claims here. Firstly, music histories draw primarily on the prestige of works, and in turn serve to consolidate that prestige. Secondly, thanks to the handing down of this prestige, an abstract entity which is 'actualised' from time to time in performance, musical practice is given a continuity that it would not possess if it relied solely on success in performance – i.e. in this case the abstract is thoroughly concrete in its consequences. Thirdly, esoteric works seldom gain prestige unless other works by the same composer have had success in performance: in all probability, even those historians who despised Schoenberg's works on aesthetic grounds would never have taken them as seriously as they did if it had not been for the triumph of the *Gurrelieder*.

The methods that have been suggested for reconstructing the reception history of musical works or groups of works differ less in the material they refer to (there is practically no getting round nineteenth- and twentieth-century music journalism) than in the cognitive goals they pose and the accents they stress. At the moment it is not even clear what, precisely, the history of musical reception means in the first place. Even so, a conviction seems to be spreading that accounts and opinions, which can be collected *ad infinitum*, can be explained and classified according to relevance if we relate them to prevailing norms, the validity of which is conditioned and delimited by the so-called 'three dimensions' of history: time, social stratum, and regional or ethnic origin.

It would seem that little use has been made till now of the possibilities latent in journalistic sources for observing the origin, consolidation and spread of those opinions and modes of reception that were later turned by history – or by 'higher criticism', as it was known in the nineteenth century – into a canon. Music historians are evidently loth to be reminded of the journalistic antecedents of their own work, and for this reason shrink from studying them for fear of weakening the prejudiced notion that history links up directly with the musical events of the past. Unless reception historians reflect upon their criteria of selection they are even more likely than their colleagues to be buried in the rubble of their source material. If they were to direct their attention to the formation of this canon they might use, as a criterion for selecting documents, the role that a given piece of evidence played in the creation of what was later to be accepted and dutifully handed down as the verdict of 'History'. Here the key problem faced by the reception historian would lie in reconstructing the causes that led some of the conflicting opinions (say as regards Beethoven's late string quartets, Liszt's tone poems or Schoenberg's atonal piano pieces) to win out in the end, and others to perish.

If, rather than discussing the formation of the canon (i.e. the transition from journalism to historiography) we wished to depict the panoply of opinion that characterised a particular period, our criterion of selection might consist in the weight that attached to an opinion by virtue of the newspaper or journal in which it appeared or the prestige of the critic who wrote it. From this standpoint Hugo Wolf's music criticism, for instance, would be of minor importance to reception history. Any reception historian writing an overview of a period would then look to find explanations for the documents that he was drawing upon primarily in the many intellectual and social currents, some coexisting peaceably, some in mutual conflict, that went to make up that confused mass which used to be apostrophised as the 'spirit of the age' – a spirit whose 'intrinsic unity' is nothing but a fabrication on the part of philosophers of history with their mania for simplification.

The reception history of works of music is determined in no small measure by the emergence of fixed, perpetually recurring clichés which, owing to the relative independence of their existence and influence, can be extracted from the context of intellectual or social history and studied in isolation.[2] Yet even the most cursory reflection is enough to show that the clichés associated with major composers, works or oeuvres differ fundamentally and profoundly from each other, not only in their actual content but also in the very way they function as *topoi* or stereotyped opinions. Eggebrecht, for instance, has shown how, in the case of Beethoven, certain catchphrases such as 'per aspera ad astra', annunciations of utopian import and figures of thought from secularised Christology were repeated *ad nauseam* without, however, losing their positive connotations. On the other hand, in Wagner criticism of the nineteenth and early twentieth centuries, the standard clichés – Wagner as the scourge of opera, the heroic innovator or the founder of a religion of art – already existed, but not the judgments and opinions associated with them. No critic has ever seriously denied the formidable impact of Wagner's achievements, and yet – as Susanna Grossmann-Vendrey's studies demonstrated – it is possible to see and condemn the foundation of Bayreuth and all its nationalist pomp as mere pretension, the mythic entanglements of the psyche in the *Ring* as a challenge on the part of liberalism, the religion of art in *Parsifal* as a vitiation of authentic Christianity, and the intellectualism of the leitmotive technique as a breach of the classicist aesthetic, one of whose basic precepts is that for art to be true to its nature it must remain concealed. The clichés remained essentially the same as before, but, in contrast to those associated with Beethoven, they reappeared in extremely changeable light. The reception of Mahler is different again. Here the contrasting judgments associated with the recurrent clichés not only accentuated the moral, religious or aesthetic significance of his symphonies, whether positively or negatively; they also touched upon their historical stature – which not even detractors as vituperative as

[2] Cf. Eggebrecht, *Zur Geschichte der Beethoven-Rezeption.*

Hanslick or Kalbeck dared to question in the case of Wagner's music dramas. For example, one of the ineradicable clichés of Mahler criticism, his juxtaposition of 'sublimity' and 'banality', has been interpreted by polemicists to mean that Mahler was unable to realise his intentions properly, and by apologists to mean that he was indifferent to his thematic material as opposed to the function it serves within the form; it has even been taken to mean that he 'rescued inferior music' and represents an 'aesthetic prefiguration' of the future reconciliation of society. Not only that, these interpretations are supposed to help us decide whether Mahler's symphonies are to stand alongside or even above those of Bruckner, or whether they represent a kind of 'bandmaster music' desperately trying to flee its own shadow.

There is no overlooking the fact that the study of clichés or *topoi* has its origins in the investigation of European literature for survivals from Antiquity and medieval Latin culture. Consequently, its emphasis lies on that part of received tradition that has managed to withstand all changes of *Zeitgeist*. If, however, we present the history of music reception from the standpoint of changes in function, just the opposite happens, and the main focus falls on the modifications, discontinuities and revised meanings that pieces of music underwent in the course of their subsequent history, which may have extended over centuries. Change in function and the handing down of a cliché are opposite sides of the same coin.

One method for grouping phenomena that might open up paths for analysis could proceed from a distinction put forward by Umberto Eco in his proposed aesthetics of architecture: the distinction between primary and secondary function.[3] By 'primary function' Eco means the utility value of a work, by 'secondary function' its symbolic value (a throne, for instance, is both something to sit on and a symbol of power). Eco shows that, not infrequently, the one function changes independently of the other: utility is exchangeable without affecting meaning and *vice versa*. To choose an example from music, the liturgical function of a church cantata is lost in concert performance, but the allegorical and religious significance of the music in relation to the text still remains intact, if diminished. Similarly, a march forfeits some of its utility value when performed at a park concert, but the military and patriotic connotations associated with the music remain unaffected by the change or loss of function.

---

[3] *Einführung in die Semiotik*, p. 312.

The opposite process, in which utility value survives while symbolic value perishes, is one of vitiation. A national anthem that no longer kindles patriotic sentiments as such but, at the most, the memory of such sentiments has left its music behind as an empty husk, its ritual application devoid of meaning. The anthem becomes its own death's-head.

At times both primary and secondary functions are lost and yet the piece is still handed down, as it has acquired new functions in the interim. A sixteenth-century sarabande performed in a concert of early music is not intended to be dance music, nor is anything left of the lascivious flavour that once characterised this genre (instead, paradoxically, this once provocative dance approaches the church music of the time, owing to its slow tempo). What Besseler called 'everyday music' has now become 'presentation music', and the symbolic value that it retains after its change of function resides in the very concept of 'early music', i.e. in that aura of the antique that gives this music its aesthetic charm. Whenever the original primary function is replaced by another the secondary function is almost always affected as well. The use of a Rachmaninov piano concerto in a film-score will not leave the connotations of the music untouched, and it would even appear that the semantic changes or accretions to the work remain even after it has returned to the concert hall.

Another method of reception history is conceivable, in addition to the study of *topoi* through analysis of literary evidence and the description of changes in function based on chronicle entries. This third method proceeds from musical source material and to a certain extent follows the same path as textual criticism, albeit in the opposite direction. Whereas the aim of textual criticism in music is to forge through the rubble of tradition and arrive at an authentic version of a work, reception history makes use of inauthentic versions, the very refuse left behind by source criticism, in order to show how later generations, whether deliberately or unwittingly, rectified texts after having discovered puzzling features in their original constitution.

However, reception history will have precious little material to work with so long as textual criticism proceeds from the assumption that it is pointless to discuss inauthentic versions because they have no bearing on the edited text. We might argue that since textual critics are forced in any case to examine the entire corpus of source material they might just as well describe and classify works that fall foul of tradition critique in point of authenticity, purely for the

benefit of reception history, i.e. from a sort of methodological al-
truism. On the other hand, many reception historians surely go too
far when, with missionary zeal for their own ancillary discipline,
they dispense with the authentic version (i.e. the one coinciding
with the composer's intentions) as representing the ultimate court
of appeal and instead postulate the existence of 'historical legitimation' whereby primacy attaches not to versions which are original
but to those which had the greatest impact on history. True, not all
periods or genres will admit of composers' intentions to which the
historian can refer. The idea of an 'authentic version' completely
evaporates in the case of folksong, or even of *Gebrauchsmusik* –
which was recast for each new performance, the first performance
having no particular precedence over later ones. Yet the musical
legacy of those centuries that based their theory of art on notion of
originality is still a legitimate object for the investigations of
textual criticism. Reception history will never supplant textual
criticism here.

Bibliography

Adler, Guido, *Der Stil in der Musik* (Leipzig, 1911, 2nd edn 1929). Drawing on Alois Riegl's notion of the 'will to style' (which in turn ties in with the *Jugendstil* of the turn of the century), Adler, around 1900, expounded his concept of style as a key criterion for histories which attribute music an independent, self-contained evolution, analogous to that of a living organism.

Methode der Musikgeschichte (Leipzig, 1919).

Adorno, Theodor W., *Ästhetische Theorie* (Frankfurt am Main, 1970).

Philosophie der neuen Musik (Tübingen, 1949, 2nd edn 1958), tr. as *Philosophy of Modern Music* (New York, 1973). Adorno interpreted the New Music of the twentieth century as expressing 'proclivities in the material', with Schoenberg and Stravinsky as antipodes. By 'material' he meant not an acoustical system given by nature but rather a distillation of historically conditioned relations existing between notes, relations which bear the imprint of past music in its entirety.

Ambros, August Wilhelm, *Geschichte der Musik* (Breslau, 1862–78).

Baur, Ferdinand Christian, *Die Epochen der kirchlichen Geschichtsschreibung* (Tübingen, 1852).

Bekker, Paul, *Richard Wagner. Das Leben im Werke* (Stuttgart, 1924), tr. as *Richard Wagner, His Life in His work* (London, 1931).

Bernhard, Christoph, 'Tractatus compositionis augmentatus', in Joseph Müller-Blattau, *Die Kompositionslehre Heinrich Schützens in der Fassung seines Schülers Christoph Bernhard* (Leipzig, 1926), pp. 40–131.

Bernheim, Ernst, *Lehrbuch der historischen Methode* (Leipzig, 1889).

Besseler, Heinrich, 'Grundfragen der Musikästhetik', *Jahrbuch der Musikbibliothek Peters*, 32 (1925), pp. 63–80.

Betti, Emilio, *Teoria generale della interpretazione* (Milan, 1955). Betti's hermeneutics are an even-handed summary of the problems, methods and trends developed in the theory of *Verstehen* or interpretation within history, law, text criticism and the arts.

Bloch, Ernst, *Geist der Utopie* (Munich, 1918). Bloch's work, which was equally inspired by Marx and by Jewish messianism, imparts philosophical form to the expressionism of its day. Its central chapter, a metaphysics and historiology of music, has had a far-reaching influence on musical thought in recent decades, culminating in the philosophical readings of Wagner in post-1950 Bayreuth productions.

Das Prinzip Hoffnung (Frankfurt am Main, 1959).

Braudel, Fernand, 'Histoire et sciences sociales', *Annales*, 13 (1958), pp. 725–33.

Burckhardt, Jacob, *Der Kultur der Renaissance in Italien* (Leipzig, 1860), tr. as *The Civilisation of the Renaissance in Italy* (London, 1878).

Weltgeschichtliche Betrachtungen, ed. R. Stadelmann (Pfullingen, 1949), tr. as *Reflections on History* (London, 1943).

Burney, Charles, *A General History of Music* (London, 1782–9).

Busoni, Ferruccio, *Entwurf einer neuen Ästhetik der Tonkunst* (Trieste, 1907, rev. Leipzig, 1916), tr. as *Sketch of a New Aesthetic of Music* (New York, 1911).

Collingwood, R. G., *An Autobiography* (London, 1939). Collingwood maintains that to understand a text we must reconstruct the question it was meant to answer. This thesis, together with his insight that historical documents are as much a part of the present as they are evidence from the past, forms one of the basic premises of an historical method that has disburdened itself of a number of nineteenth-century prejudices.

Danto, Arthur C., *Analytical Philosophy of History* (Cambridge, 1965). Danto's theory applies the analytic philosophy of language to the writing of history, elaborating the notion that, since historical events and processes are always revealed and handed down in the form of propositions, we must, to understand history, analyse the language in which it is documented.

Dilthey, Wilhelm, *Der Aufbau der geschichtlichen Welt in den Geisteswissenschaften* (Berlin, 1910), repr. in *Gesammelte Schriften*, vol. 7 (Leipzig, 1923, rev. Stuttgart, 1958), tr. as *Pattern and Meaning in History* (London, 1961). By juxtaposing *Verstehen* and *Erklären* Dilthey hoped, in answer to Kant's *Critique of Pure Reason* with its orientation on the natural sciences, to found a 'critique of historical reason' as a basis for the humanities. Though increasingly the object of scepticism in recent decades, his view nevertheless figured prominently in German music histories between 1920 and 1950, and is hence deserving of historical attention at the very least.

Droysen, Johann Gustav, *Historik*, ed. R. Hübner (3rd edn, Munich, 1958). Droysen's book is compiled from a lecture series delivered in 1857. Today, a full century later, it is still a basic work on the historical method, its presentation of the problems remaining vital even if its proposed solutions are no longer entirely tenable.

Texte zur Geschichtstheorie, ed. G. Birtsch and J. Rüsen (Göttingen, 1972).

Eco, Umberto, *Einführung in die Semiotik* (Munich, 1972), tr. as *A Theory of Semiotics* (Bloomington, Ind., 1976).

Eggebrecht, Hans Heinrich, *Zur Geschichte der Beethoven-Rezeption* (Mainz, 1972).

Eichenbaum, Boris, *Aufsätze zur Theorie und Geschichte der Literatur* (Frankfurt am Main, 1965).

Einstein, Alfred, *Greatness in Music* (New York, 1941).

Ellis, Alexander John, 'Tonometrical Observations in Some Existing Non-Harmonic Musical Scales', *Proceedings of the Royal Society*, 37 (1884), pp. 368–85.

Engels, Friedrich, and Karl Marx, *Über Kunst und Literatur*, ed. M. Lifschitz (Berlin, 1953), tr. as *On Literature and Art* (Moscow, 1976).

Fétis, François-Joseph, *Traité complet de la théorie et de la pratique de l'harmonie* (Paris, 1844).

Fichte, Johann Gottlieb, *Die Grundzüge des gegenwärtigen Zeitalters* (Berlin, 1806), tr. as *The Characteristics of the Present Age* (London, 1847).

Forkel, Johann Nicolaus, *Allgemeine Geschichte der Musik* (Leipzig, 1788–1801). A universal history of music which, however, breaks off in the sixteenth century. Forkel, a noted biographer of Bach, clearly illustrates an idea expounded in the introduction, namely that it is the evolution of 'avenues of expression' in music – in which expressive and logical dimensions complement and enhance one another – that forms the actual content of music history as a process directed towards an ultimate goal.

Freyer, Hans, *Weltgeschichte Europas* (2nd edn, Stuttgart, 1954).

Freytag, Gustav, *Bilder aus der deutschen Vergangenheit* (Leipzig, 1859), tr. as *Pictures of German Life in the 15th, 16th and 17th Centuries* (London, 1962).

Gadamer, Hans-Georg, *Wahrheit und Methode* (Tübingen, 1960), tr. as *Truth and Method* (London, 1975). Gadamer's proposed 'outline of a philosophical hermeneutics', as his subtitle reads, has had an extraordinary influence on text critics and historians, due partly to his theory of historical impact and partly to his rehabilitation of tradition, and of prejudice, as conditions for the proper understanding of a text.

Glareanus, Henricus Loritus, *Dodecachordon* (Basle, 1547, repr. New York, 1965).

Grossmann-Vendrey, Susanna, *Bayreuth in der deutschen Presse* (Regensburg, 1977).

Grout, Donald Jay, *A History of Western Music* (New York, 1962).

Habermas, Jürgen, *Erkenntnis und Interesse* (Frankfurt am Main, 1968), tr. as *Knowledge and Human Interests* (London, 1972).

Zur Logik der Sozialwissenschaften (Tübingen, 1967).

Handschin, Jacques, *Musikgeschichte im Überblick* (Lucerne, 1948). A majestic 'survey' by a great scholar with an original turn of mind. Handschin's history is the only book which consistently implements the principle that past ages of music, the thirteenth century no less than the nineteenth, must be treated as equal and allowed to come into their own.

Hanslick, Eduard, *Vom Musikalisch-Schönen* (Leipzig, 1854), tr. as *The Beautiful in Music* (London, 1891).

Hawkins, John, *A General History of the Science and Practice of Music* (London, 1776). Together with Burney and Forkel, Hawkins was the founder of a universal history of music which – unlike nineteenth-century historicism – held that there is such a thing as Absolute Beauty, which is gradually realised and brought to light by the evolutionary course of history.

Hegel, Georg Wilhelm Friedrich, *Die Vernunft in der Geschichte*, ed. G. Lasson (Leipzig, 1917).

Heidegger, Martin, *Sein und Zeit* (8th edn. Tübingen, 1957), tr. as *Being and Time* (London, 1962).

Helmholtz, Hermann von, *Die Lehre von den Tonempfindungen* (Braunschweig, 1863), tr. as *On the Sensations of Tone as a Physiological Basis for the Theory of Music* (London, 1875).

Herder, Johann Gottfried, *Auch eine Philosophie der Geschichte zur Bildung der Menschheit*, ed. H.-G. Gadamer (Frankfurt am Main, 1967).

Heuss, Alfred, *Verlust der Geschichte* (Göttingen, 1959).

Hoffmann, Ernst Theodor Amadeus, *Schriften zur Musik*, ed. F. Schnapp (Munich, 1963).

Huizinga, Johan, *Das Problem der Renaissance* (Darmstadt, 1971).

Humboldt, Wilhelm von, 'Über die Aufgabe des Geschichtsschreibers', in *Werke*, vol. 1 (Darmstadt, 1960), pp. 596 ff.

Jauss, Hans Robert, 'Geschichte der Kunst und Historie', in *Geschichte – Ereignis und Erzählung*, ed. R. Koselleck (Munich, 1973), pp. 175–209.

'Racines und Goethes Iphigenie', in *Rezeptionsästhetik*, ed. R. Warning (Munich, 1975).

Kalbeck, Max, *Gereimtes und Ungereimtes* (Berlin, 1885).

Kracauer, Siegfried, *Geschichte – Vor den letzten Dingen* (Frankfurt am Main, 1971).

Kuhn, Thomas, *The Structure of Scientific Revolutions* (Chicago, 1963, rev. 1970). Kuhn advances a theory of 'paradigms' and 'changes of paradigms' whereby, in the natural sciences, the continuity of research is broken from time to time by an abrupt exchange of axiomatic systems. This thesis has been adopted by cultural historians and transferred with great profit from the history of physics to the history of aesthetics where, for instance, the idea of 'absolute music' is taken in Kuhn's sense to be a paradigm, namely the prevailing paradigm of the nineteenth century.

Lippman, Edward A., 'Stil', in *Musik in Geschichte und Gegenwart*, vol. 12 (Kassel, 1965).

Ludwig, Friedrich, 'Die geistliche nichtliturgische, weltliche einstimmige und die mehrstimmige Musik des Mittelalters bis zum Anfang des 15. Jahrhunderts', in *Handbuch der Musikgeschichte*, ed. G. Adler, vol. 1 (Munich, 1977), pp. 157–295.

Marx, Adolf Bernhard, *Die Musik des 19. Jahrhunderts und ihre Plefge* (Leipzig, 1855).

Marx, Karl, *Frühschriften*, ed. S. Landshut (Stuttgart, 1964).

Theories of Surplus Value (London, 1951).

Zur Kritik der politischen Ökonomie (Berlin, 1859), tr. as *A Contribution to the Critique of Political Economy* (New York, 1904). The introduction to this work, which discusses the relation between 'base' and 'superstructure', 'being' and 'consciousness', figures alongside the chapter on the 'Fetish Character of Commodities' from *Das Kapital* and several passages from Marx's early writings as a 'classic text' for the non-economists among Marxists.

see also Engels, Friedrich

Mattheson, Johann, *Der vollkommene Capellmeister* (Hamburg, 1739).

Nietzsche, Friedrich, *Die Geburt der Tragödie aus dem Geiste der Musik* (Leipzig, 1872), tr. as *The Birth of Tragedy* (New York, 1967).

Unzeitgemässe Betrachtungen (Leipzig, 1876), tr. as *Thoughts out of Season* (London, 1909). Nietzsche's impact has been incalculable. In musicology, it resides in a latent distrust of a form of 'history' which is debilitating to 'life' (*Von Nutzen und Nachteil der Historie für das Leben*, Basle, 1949); in the permanent mark he left on aesthetics with his categories 'Apollonian' and 'Dionysiac' (*The Birth of Tragedy*); and in a criticism of Wagner turning from initial veneration to hatred (or consisting of veneration and hatred in equal measure), the influence of which is detectable in writers as recent as Thomas Mann and Theodor Adorno.

Novalis (Friedrich von Hardenburg), *Fragmente*, ed. E. Kamnitzer (Dresden, 1929).

Pinder, Wilhelm, *Das Problem der Generation in der Kunstgeschichte Europas* (Munich, 1961).

Ranke, Leopold von, *Tagebuchblätter* (Leipzig, 1890).

Rickert, Heinrich, *Kulturwissenschaft und Naturwissenschaft* (6th edn, Tübingen, 1926), tr. as *Science and History* (Princeton, N.J., 1962).

Riehl, Wilhelm Heinrich, *Hausmusik* (Leipzig, 1855).

Riemann, Hugo, *Handbuch der Musikgeschichte* (Leipzig, 1904–13, 2nd edn 1922).

Rothacker, Erich, *Logik und Systematik der Geisteswissenschaften* (Munich, 1965).

Schiller, Friedrich, 'Über naive und sentimentalische Dichtung', in *Werke*, vol. 20, ed. B. von Wiese (Weimar, 1962), pp. 413–503.

Schleiermacher, Friedrich, *Hermeneutik*, ed. H. Kimmerle (Heidelberg, 1959).

Schoenberg, Arnold, 'Brahms the Progressive', in *Style and Idea* (London, 1975), pp. 398–441.

Schopenhauer, Arthur, *Die Welt als Wille und Vorstellung*, vol. 1 (Leipzig, 1819), tr. as *The World as Will and Representation*, vol. 1 (New York, 1969).

Schumann, Robert, *Gesammelte Schriften über Musik und Musiker* (1854), ed. M. Kreisig (Leipzig, 1914), tr. as *Music and Musicians* (London, 1877).

Shklovsky, Victor, *O teorii prozy* (Moscow, 1925), tr. as *Theorie der Prosa* (Frankfurt am Main, 1966). The Russian formalists maintain that the effect of art resides in the conspicuousness of its artifices, and that as these artifices recede a corresponding urge toward change – i.e. historical progress – arises. This thesis can be used as a premise on which to base an intrinsic history of art, independent of social or cultural history and bearing out the full historiographical consequences of the principle of aesthetic autonomy.

Spitta, Philipp, 'Kunstwissenschaft und Kunst', in *Zur Musik* (Berlin, 1892), pp. 1–14. Spitta, a noted biographer of Bach and, alongside Ambros, Chrysander and Adler, one of the nineteenth-century founders of musicology, made a rigorous distinction between studying the 'being' of music, which falls to the part of aesthetics, and studying its 'becoming', which is the task of history. In other words, unlike historicists who conceive of music as being what Adorno called 'historical through and through', he saw in written history only a reconstruction of the conditions of art, not a key to its essence.

Tieck, Johann Ludwig, 'Phantasien über die Kunst', in Wilhelm Heinrich Wackenroder, *Werke und Briefe* (Heidelberg, 1967), tr. as *Wilhelm Heinrich Wackenroder's Confessions and Fantasies* (University Park, Pa., 1971).

Troeltsch, Ernst, *Der Historismus und seine Probleme* (Tübingen, 1922).

Uffenbach, Johann Friedrich von, 'Reisentagebuch', in Eberhard Preussner, *Die musikalischen Reisen des Herrn von Uffenbach* (Kassel, 1949).

Vodička, Felix, 'Die Konkretisation des literarischen Werks', in *Rezeptionsästhetik*, ed. R. Warning (Munich, 1975).

Weber, Max, *Die rationalen und soziologischen Grundlagen der Musik* (Munich, 1921), tr. as *The Rational and Social Foundations of Music* (Carbondale, Ill., 1958). Weber's proposition that Western music has evolved in a process of increasing rationality has, since his death, become one of those ideas of which it can be said that they not merely reflect history but take an active part within it.

Gesammelte Aufsätze zur Wissenschaftslehre (Tübingen, 1958).

Weimann, Robert, *Literaturgeschichte und Mythologie* (Leipzig, 1971).

Werckmeister, Otto Karl, *Ideologie und Kunst bei Marx* (Frankfurt am Main, 1974).

Wilamowitz-Möllendorf, Ulrich von, *Zukunftsphilologie* (Berlin, 1872).

Winckelmann, Johann Joachim, *Kleine Schriften*, ed. W. Rehm (Berlin, 1968).

Windelband, Wilhelm, 'Geschichte und Naturwissenschaft', in *Präludien*, vol. 2 (Tübingen, 1919), pp. 136–60. Windelband distinguished between the 'nomothetic' natural sciences and the 'idiographic' cultural sciences, claiming that written history consists in the description of things that are particular and non-recurring. This distinction was shaken long ago by the proof that the depiction of individual occurrences and the discovery or construction of general laws are mutually conditioned. Nevertheless, it has held its place in the scholarly parlance of historians and text critics.

Wölfflin, Heinrich, *Kunstgeschichtliche Grundbegriffe* (Munich, 1915).

Index

abstraction, dangers of, 29ff
Adler, Guido, 14ff
Adorno, Theodor, 29ff, 61, 64, 77, 106, 113f, 129
aesthetic autonomy: as basis of history of works, 12; antithetic to history, 19f; attacked by social historians, 27f; as historical fact, 28; definition and history of, 109ff; and value-judgments, 110; limitations as historiographic axiom, 112; as moral precept, 113f; Marxist dual meaning of 114f; and *Zeitgeist*, 143; as key category in 19th-century music, 144ff; vs. art for art's sake, 146
aesthetic presence: as basis of music history, 4ff; absence from political history, 35
'aestheticising' the historical, 71
affections, doctrine of, 21
Ambros, August Wilhelm, 131
anthropocentric constants, 52f
anthropology and tradition critique, 54f
Aristotle, 4, 40, 76, 142
art history: as contradiction in terms, 25, 32; as chain of mutual influence, 25
artificial music: significance of musical work in, 6f; authority of text in, 28
'authority principle' of meaning, 159f
autonomisation of early music, 111, 116

Bach, C. P. E., 34, 157
Bach, J. S., 5, 9f, 28, 49, 62, 67, 75, 92, 95f, 98, 100, 111, 157, 160
base–superstructure schema: philistinism of, 108; and aesthetic autonomy, 115f; as final arbiter in history, 119f; relevance to art history, 120
Baur, Ferdinand Christian, 54
Beethoven, Ludwig van, 9, 22, 31, 32, 37, 40, 49f, 67, 69, 92, 95f, 100, 117f, 120, 139f, 148, 157, 161f
Bekker, Paul, 22
Benjamin, Walter, 155

Berlioz, Hector, 49f, 160
Bernhard, Christoph, 20, 148
Bernheim, Ernst, 1
Besseler, Heinrich, 71, 108f, 139, 164
Bildung in 19th-century music, 146f
biography: idealistic vs. realistic, 26; as narrative model, 26f, 45; documentary, 34
Bloch, Ernst, 7, 66, 112, 134
Brahms, Johannes, 31, 50, 69, 103, 133, 157
Braudel, Fernand, 142
Bruckner, Anton, 157f, 163
Burckhardt, Jacob, 1, 8, 51f, 79, 120f, 135
Burke, Edmund, 62
Burney, Charles, 34, 40
Busoni, Ferruccio, 8

canon of musical works, 92–109; historical or aesthetic?, 93ff; predetermined for historian, 96f; dialectical relation to historiography, 98f; origins, 99ff; and dogmatics, 101ff; and tradition critique, 105ff
carrier strata, 101
causal explanation, 83
Chopin, Frédéric, 56
'circumstances' vs. structures, 136
classicism, classical status: as normative category, 15; as stylistic label, 16f; and naturalness in music, 62; and the musical canon, 95f; as category in 19th-century music, 148f
'cogency' principle of meaning, 160
Collingwood, R. G., 153
composer as subject of history, 38
concert life, 19th-century, 148
concrete utopia (Bloch), 112
concretisation of musical works, 151, 153
conservatism in music: relation to tradition, 69; as political programme, 69f; relation to historicism, 70
continuity, concept of: in narrative history, 10f, 46; antithetic to art, 19f; derived from the novel, 47